# BUSES

## YEARBOOK 2011

### Edited by STEWART J. BROWN

First published 2010

ISBN 978 0 7110 3474 7

All rights reserved. No part of this book may be reproduced or transmitted in any form or by any means, electronic or mechanical, including photocopying, recording or by any information storage and retrieval system, without permission from the Publisher in writing.

© Ian Allan Publishing Ltd 2010

Published by Ian Allan Publishing

an imprint of Ian Allan Publishing Ltd, Hersham, Surrey, KT12 4RG.
Printed in England by Ian Allan Printing Ltd, Hersham, Surrey, KT12 4RG.

Code: 1008/E

Distributed in the United States of America and Canada by BookMasters Distribution Services

Visit the Ian Allan Publishing website at www.ianallanpublishing.com

**Copyright**
Illegal copying and selling of publications deprives authors, publishers and booksellers of income, without which there would be no investment in new publications. Unauthorised versions of publications are also likely to be inferior in quality and contain incorrect information. You can help by reporting copyright infringements and acts of piracy to the Publisher or the UK Copyright Service.

*Front cover:* **Route-branding and low-floor buses are just two of the innovations introduced to Lothian Region Transport by Neil Renilson. This Wright-bodied Volvo B9TL was new in 2009.** GAVIN BOOTH

*Back cover (upper):* **Few operators now remain in local-authority ownership. In 2002 this Alexander-bodied Volvo Citybus was painted to celebrate 90 years of municipal transport in Bournemouth, but three years later the operation was sold to Transdev.** STEWART J. BROWN

*Back cover (lower):* **Having fought hard for them 12 years earlier, Stagecoach sold its Darlington operations in 2007. Now running for Arriva, this Alexander-bodied Dart was new to Stagecoach Selkent.** GARY MITCHELHILL

*Previous page:* **Brighton & Hove's operations on the Sussex coast include the former Southdown route to Eastbourne, which offers spectacular views. A 2006 OmniDekka illustrates the point in April 2009.** MICHAEL H. C. BAKER

# Contents

**Missing municipals** — 3
*Stewart J. Brown*

**The twilight zone** — 14
*Tony Wilson*

**Deregulated? Well, yes … and no** — 20
*Alan Millar*

**Maltese mixture** — 34
*John Young*

**Municipal pride, Southern style** — 42
*Michael H. C. Baker*

**Scottish Titans** — 52
*Billy Nicol*

**Further round the bend** — 56
*Robert E. Jowitt*

**Devon and Cornwall in the 1980s** — 64
*Mark Bailey*

**Of Paramount importance** — 72
*David Jukes*

**Grand National** — 82
*Chris Drew*

**Madder and yet madder still** — 86
*Gavin Booth*

**Lancs Lynx let loose** — 96
*David Wayman*

**One, two, many** — 100
*David Cole*

**Berkhof bonanza** — 110
*Geoff Mills*

**One and only** — 116
*Tony Greaves*

**Seven decades of service** — 124
*Les Dickinson*

# Missing municipals

**Municipal buses were an identifying feature of many British towns and cities for many years. Now most have vanished. Stewart J. Brown looks back at municipal transport since deregulation.**

*All photographs by Stewart J. Brown*

THE BRITISH BUS INDUSTRY was turned upside down a quarter-century ago, when some 50-odd years of tight control on bus services was scrapped. The year was 1986. The big change was deregulation. Critics — and there are many — view October 1986 and the opening up to competition of the British bus market outside London as the end of civilisation as we knew it. Supporters, some of whom prefer the term 'commercialisation' to the more common 'deregulation', consider it the start of a bus-industry renaissance. And depending on where you look, they both might be right.

Call it what you will, the brave new world of the late 1980s involved not just the removal of restrictive legislation dating back to the 1930s but also a change in the political landscape in which, crudely, the public sector was inefficient and wasteful, and the private sector the opposite. Despite changes in government and some compelling evidence that this simplistic view might not be wholly accurate, the notion that the private sector is better able than the public sector to provide a range of essential services still prevails, a quarter of a century later.

One consequence has been a sharp decline in the number of local authorities running their own bus services. In the early 1930s there were around 100, including places where municipal buses have long been forgotten, such as Keighley and Kilmarnock. Most were Corporation Transport Departments, a few in Yorkshire were Joint Omnibus Committees, and in some parts of England and Wales there were small bus fleets run by delightfully named Urban District Councils.

Regardless of the style of ownership, the number was effectively halved in the early 1970s. This was caused largely by the creation of Passenger Transport Executives in the six biggest English conurbations and also by the amalgamation of some of the smaller municipal fleets when local government in England and Wales was reorganised in 1974. The PTEs swallowed up all the really big municipal fleets — Birmingham,

**Maidstone Borough Council's livery was, prior to deregulation, a staid combination of brown and cream, as worn by this 1978 Bedford YMT with 61-seat Duple Dominant body, seen in the town in 1987.**

**Maidstone's image was transformed when it adopted Boro'line branding. This is a Leyland Olympian with Optare bodywork, operating on a London Regional Transport contract.**

Liverpool, Manchester, Leeds, Sheffield and Glasgow. Manchester, to take one example, ran more than 1,200 buses, and the other 10 bus-operating municipalities in the Greater Manchester area ran another 1,300 between them. Municipal transport was big business.

By the time deregulation was introduced there were still 45 municipal bus fleets running year-round scheduled bus services in Britain. Today there are just 11. Britain's buses have effectively been demunicipalised.

The Transport Act 1985, which deregulated local buses, also required local authorities to reform their bus operations as limited companies. At most of them there was little external evidence of the change, although one, Maidstone, adopted a completely new identity, Boro'line, devised by the Best Impressions consultancy. Another, Lincoln, diversified into taxis, running 20 Carbodies FX4s in fleet livery. The operation lasted for three years, and was closed at the start of 1989. A few tried minibuses, usually in small numbers, although Plymouth took no fewer than 81 Dodges in 1986. Preston also invested in Dodges, taking 20 in 1987 to address competition from United Transport, which had introduced 75 minibuses to the town.

**A number of municipals ran ex-London Routemasters as a competitive tool in the deregulated era. Among them was Blackpool, which used a distinctive lined-out red and white livery for its Routemasters. It initially bought 12, and these operated on a route that was facing competition from neighbouring Fylde Borough Transport.**

A few municipals showed a new interest in coaches as a way of expanding their businesses in the late 1980s. These included Ipswich (Bantam Coaches), Grampian (Mairs), Grimsby-Cleethorpes (Peter Sheffield Coaches) Brighton (Lewes Coach Co and Campings Coaches), Fylde (Seagull Coaches), Lancaster (Lonsdale Coaches) and Rossendale (Ellen Smith Coaches). One municipal, Hull, even established a coach operation in Europe, with Voyage National running three coaches in Lille, France. Established in 1989, this was the bridgehead for further European expansion in 1990, with the purchase of the 14-vehicle Kivits Reizen in Holland. Closer to home, Hull also bought the 20-vehicle Reynard Pullman business in York. The Voyage National business was sold at the start of 1993, and shortly afterwards Hull sold its York company to Durham Travel Services.

Others established new services outside their traditional operating areas. In 1987 Leicester set up an 11-bus operation in Loughborough, marketed as Trippit, with a fleet of new Optare CityPacers; this was sold to Midland Fox in the summer of 1989. Chesterfield set up a Retford & District operation in 1988. Lincoln established Scunthorpe's Betta Bus with 19 Reeve Burgess Beaver minibuses, in response to competition in the city from Lincolnshire Road Car. Betta Bus was short-lived, closing in February 1989, after less than nine months, and the vehicles were sold.

The biggest expansion in a new area was by Boro'line Maidstone, which made a successful bid for London Transport tenders, initially in the Bexley area in 1988, but ultimately with a route into Central London. In 1986 Boro'line ran 40 buses. Four years later it was running 130. Its expansion had been rapid — as was its demise. In November 1991 the council advertised it for sale. Maidstone & District registered a competing network in Maidstone, and the whole edifice came crashing down in February 1992. Kentish Bus took over the LRT contracts and 57 buses. The receivers took over what was left of the business and kept it going until May, when M&D bought most of the assets. Not so much Boro'line as end of the line.

Redundant London Routemasters were tried by a number of operators, either as a competitive tool or as a way of raising the operator's image. Those municipals which ran Routemasters were Blackpool, Southampton, Southend and Burnley & Pendle.

**Taff-Ely took six Optare CityPacers in September 1987, as it was coming under pressure from National Welsh, one of whose Leyland Nationals, serving the same route, is seen behind in this view. Twelve months later Taff Ely's bus business was sold to National Welsh. Note the contrast between the sleek lines of the CityPacer and the shaded tramway-style numerals used for the fleet number.**

**Another casualty of National Welsh aggression was Inter Valley Link, whose fleet included this Leyland Leopard with robust-looking East Lancs body. It was one of three purchased in 1980. The fleetname is displayed in Welsh above the front wheel.**

The municipal sell-off started at the end of 1987, when Portsmouth City Transport was put up for sale. Portsmouth was a substantial operation, running 110 buses. It was announced in March 1988 that Southern Vectis was the highest bidder, but the following month the Isle of Wight company withdrew its offer, stating that PCT's finances were in a worse state than it had thought. The sale finally went ahead in June, to a consortium made up of PCT employees and Southampton CityBus — so it remained in local-authority ownership, albeit a different authority. However, that wasn't the end of the story. Stagecoach bought the company in the autumn of 1989 but had to sell it again — to Transit Holdings — at the start of 1991 after an investigation by the Monopolies & Mergers Commission.

There was an early move towards privatisation in Leicester, where the management of Leicester CityBus indicated in the summer of 1988 that it was interested in buying the business, but the council made no move to sell and retained ownership of its municipal buses. There was, however, a change of livery, from an attractive red, grey and white (the council's corporate colours) to a sombre maroon and cream, reflecting the operation's heritage through its similarity to a scheme that had last been used some 25 years previously.

The second municipal to be sold was Taff-Ely. A small operation, running just 20 buses, it was bought by National Welsh in September 1988, when the company was in expansionist mode. National Welsh would expand again in February 1989 when it took over the operations of Inter Valley Link, promptly selling most of the 83 vehicles which it acquired. Inter Valley Link was the post-1986 name for Rhymney Valley District Council's bus business.

National Welsh was in the meantime competing in Merthyr Tydfil, and in the spring of 1989 most of Merthyr Tydfil Transport's drivers defected to National Welsh. MTT kept going by using drivers borrowed from other operators. However, the business had been seriously undermined by National Welsh. In July the administrators were called in, and the business closed in the following month. It was a sad end to an operation which had worked to improve its image by investing in a fleet of 18 new Leyland Lynxes in 1987/8.

Those who viewed National Welsh as a predator no doubt thought the company got its come-uppance when it was dismembered in 1992 after the receivers were called in at the start of the year. In the early 1980s National Welsh was one of Wales's biggest operators, with 700 buses. Ten years later it had vanished without trace.

As National Welsh was disintegrating one of the surviving South Wales municipals, Cynon Valley, serving Aberdare, was sold to Western Travel, which had taken over part of the National Welsh business in 1991. So in a short space of time four municipal fleets in South Wales disappeared — Taff-Ely, Inter Valley Link, Merthyr Tydfil and Cynon Valley.

One of the biggest — and, as time would reveal, most significant — of municipal sales took place in January 1989, when Grampian Regional Transport was sold to its management and employees, for £5 million. Nobody could have guessed then that the former Aberdeen Corporation Transport Department would become a major force in the world of buses. There was just one other sale in 1989, Derby City Transport being purchased by a consortium made up of its employees and Luton & District Transport. Derby ran 135 buses. In 1994 Luton & District was bought by British Bus, and Derby City Transport became a British Bus subsidiary.

**In the early 1980s Grampian Regional Transport had run joint services with the Scottish Bus Group's Northern subsidiary, but upon deregulation the two businesses became competitors. The standard Grampian bus of the 1980s was the Leyland Olympian with Alexander body, and this one is operating to Stonehaven, in what had traditionally been Northern territory. The Northern Olympian in the background is competing with Grampian on an Aberdeen city service.**

One English municipal business closed in 1989. Barrow Borough Transport had been offered for sale in January, but its services were facing stiff competition from Ribble. In May Ribble was acquired by Stagecoach, which the following month took over BBT's operations and some of its vehicles.

There was just one sale in 1990, of Chesterfield Transport to its management and employees. That was followed in 1991 by Cleveland Transit and Tayside, both also sold to management/employee buy-out teams. Both Chesterfield and Cleveland would subsequently be sold on to Stagecoach, while Tayside would later be purchased by National Express. Also sold in 1991 was Lincoln City Transport, in which management and employees took a 60% stake, the balance being owned by Derby City Transport. In February 1993 the Lincoln business was bought by Yorkshire Traction (owner of Lincolnshire Road Car), and the two operations were soon merged.

There was a flurry of activity in 1993. Five municipal bus businesses were sold to management/employee buy-outs — Preston in April, Hartlepool in June and Brighton, Fylde and Southampton in December. Also in December, Kingston-upon-Hull City Transport was bought by a consortium comprising the company's employees and Cleveland Transit, which had been privatised two years earlier. The Kivits Reizen coach business in Holland was sold

*Right:* **Barrow Borough Transport vanished without trace in 1989 after facing strong competition from Ribble. This is a 1987 view of a smartly presented Leyland National, one of five purchased in 1974.**

*Left:* **Fylde expanded its operations in Blackpool after deregulation, using new minibuses and assorted second-hand vehicles. Already well past its first flush of youth when acquired by Fylde in 1987 was this ex-Grimsby-Cleethorpes Daimler Fleetline/Roe, new in 1971. It is seen still in its original owner's colours, rendering Fylde's 'Blue Buses' fleetname somewhat incongruous.**

*Right:* **Cleveland Transit was sold to its management and employees in 1991. Its livery was a crisp combination of green, white and yellow, an update of its previous green and yellow scheme. Pictured in Stockton is a 1970 Leyland Atlantean PDR1A/1 which had been rebodied in 1986 by Northern Counties.**

**Hull's municipal buses had been blue and white, and when purchased by Cleveland Transit in 1993 Kingston-upon-Hull City Transport introduced a blue-based version of the Transit livery. A 1988 Dennis Dominator with Alexander-style East Lancs bodywork shows the short-lived colour scheme. Along with Transit, KHCT was acquired by Stagecoach in 1994.**

to its employees, bringing to an end KHCT's Continental adventures. KHCT would adopt an attractive blue, white and yellow livery in the same style as Cleveland's green, white and yellow. Fylde's sojourn in the private sector would be brief. Just five months after its buy-out it found itself back in public ownership — in the hands of Blackpool Transport, which would run it as a separate business until 1996.

In 1993 British Bus bought two municipal operations, both of them in Essex — Southend in June, followed by Colchester in November — and giving it a presence in what was then Badgerline country. In the same year Grampian, which had been privatised at the start of 1989, purchased its first bus operations south of the border — Northampton Transport in October, followed by Leicester CityBus in November. Both adopted Grampian's corporate livery of cream with a stronger two-tone relief colour, in this case red.

The other big Scottish group, Stagecoach, was also active in the English municipal market in 1993. Its first involvement was in Lancaster. The council had intended to sell the Lancaster City Transport business on the open market but in May accepted a bid from Stagecoach — not for the company but for around a dozen of its 93 vehicles and most of its services. Before making its offer Stagecoach had registered its own route network in the city — a move which reduced the value of the LCT business to any other would-be buyers. Not for the first — or last — time, Stagecoach's dealings attracted the attention of the Monopolies & Mergers Commission. LCT's Lonsdale Coaches business, with 12 vehicles, was purchased by local coach operator Shaw Hadwin.

In November 1993 Stagecoach also bought Grimsby-Cleethorpes Transport, its first municipal purchase since its brief ownership of Portsmouth City Transport in 1989/90. It would add to its portfolio of former municipal bus companies in 1994 when it purchased two businesses which had each been the subject of a management buy-out — Cleveland Transit, which brought with it the erstwhile Kingston-upon-Hull City Transport business, and Hartlepool Transport, which had been independent for just under 18 months. Chesterfield Transport followed in 1995 after reports that Mainline had been planning to buy it.

But it was in Darlington that Stagecoach hit the headlines. In a move which had echoes of events in Barrow in 1989 and Lancaster in 1993, Stagecoach effectively ran Darlington Transport off the road in 1994. In July the council had indicated its intention to sell the company, and in October it named three short-listed bidders, Badgerline, Stagecoach and Yorkshire

**Darlington Transport was effectively run off the road by Stagecoach in 1994. Seen in the late 1980s is one of eight Seddon Pennine RUs, with 47-seat dual-door Pennine bodywork, dating from the winter of 1973/4. The bus carries a prominent sign advising that smoking is not allowed, at a time when it was still common practice to allow passengers to smoke on buses.**

Traction, the last-named being the preferred bidder. Then, in November, Stagecoach launched free bus services in the town, whereupon Yorkshire Traction, not surprisingly, withdrew its bid. Very quickly Darlington Transport went into administration, and its services ceased. Its 29 buses were sold at auction, and its small coach operation was sold to J&C Coaches of Newton Aycliffe.

There was smoother expansion by Stagecoach in 1996, in East Lancashire. In March it acquired Pendle council's share of Burnley & Pendle Transport. Burnley Council had not wanted to sell but bowed to the inevitable and sold its stake to Stagecoach in November. Meanwhile nearby Hyndburn sold its bus business to Stagecoach in September. Given that Stagecoach already owned Ribble, the acquisition of the two municipal business strengthened the group's position in East Lancashire — although it would later pull out, selling its operations in Burnley, Pendle, Hyndburn and Blackburn to Blazefield.

Also in 1996 FirstBus — formed the previous year by the merger of GRT and Badgerline — consolidated its position in East Anglia with the purchase of Great Yarmouth Transport. The 51-bus operation was branded Blue Bus and placed under the control of the group's Eastern Counties business. At that time First had yet to adopt a corporate livery.

In 1997 a couple of the early-1990s buy-outs of municipal fleets sold out to the big groups, Southampton going to FirstBus and Brighton to Go-Ahead.

At the start of the new millennium the number of municipally owned bus operations in Britain had fallen from 45 in 1986 to just 17, and during the first decade of the 21st century another six would go. One of those which survived, Nottingham City Transport, saw some private-sector investment, French group Transdev taking an 18% stake in the business. Transdev also operates the city's trams.

Transdev extended its municipal bus interests in 2005 when it took over Bournemouth Transport. The local council had announced in December 2004 that it intended to sell the company, then took almost three months to set the process in motion. In the summer it announced that Transdev was the successful bidder — only to have the sale blocked by the Department for Transport after a suggestion that the council may have acted unlawfully by setting rules for the sale which excluded local coach operator Excelsior from making a bid. Excelsior had complained about the bidding rules, which required that private companies submitting bids should have assets of £5 million, while public companies were required to have assets of only £500,000. Bidding was then reopened, but in the end Transdev remained the preferred bidder and took over the business almost 12 months after its sale had first been mooted. The council retained a 10% stake in the company.

In January 2007 Transdev acquired another municipal bus business, Blackburn Borough Transport. Transdev already had operations in the area — the Lancashire United company acquired 12 months earlier with the Blazefield group, which included the former municipal bus operations at Hyndburn and Burnley & Pendle. The Blackburn

*Above:* **Following a management-led employee buy-out, in 1993, Hartlepool Transport enjoyed 18 months of independence, which ended when the business was sold to Stagecoach in 1994. The Hartlepool fleet included some elderly vehicles, such as this 1972 Bristol RE, seen shortly after the Stagecoach takeover.**

*Left:* **Stagecoach acquired the Burnley & Pendle business in two stages in 1996, buying first Pendle Council's share and then Burnley's. One of 10 ECW-bodied Bristol VRTs purchased by Burnley & Pendle in 1978 is seen approaching Burnley town centre 10 years later.**

*Left:* **Another of Stagecoach's East Lancashire purchases in 1996 was that of Hyndburn Borough Transport. The fleet used a distinctive colour scheme of dark blue and red, as shown on an ex-Greater Manchester PTE Atlantean/ Northern Counties in Accrington in 1988.**

**Bournemouth celebrated 90 years of municipal transport in 2002, as proclaimed by this Alexander-bodied Volvo Citybus, one of five delivered in 1989. A 1978 Fleetline, also bodied by Alexander and looking good for a 24-year-old bus, pulls out to pass. The town's municipal bus operation would not survive to celebrate its centenary, being sold to Transdev in 2005.**

operations were absorbed into Lancashire United, and in the summer of 2007 key local services were rebranded 'SpotOn'.

Meanwhile, in July 2006, Chester City Council had decided to sell its bus operation, setting in train a chain of events it did not anticipate. Arriva offered to buy the business — but at the same time registered a competing service network. The Council took action in the High Court, demanding that Arriva de-register its Chester network. It was a long-drawn-out process, and in June 2007, just as Arriva won the High Court action, First sneaked in under Arriva's nose and did a deal with the council — which clearly had fallen out with Arriva — to buy the company. As in Bournemouth, albeit for different reasons, the sale of Chester's bus company took the best part of 12 months.

The next to fall was Eastbourne, the world's first municipal bus operator, having commenced operations in 1903. The council had sold a minority stake to Kéolis in 2000, but in November 2008 Stagecoach took over the whole business. Go-Ahead, heir to the municipal bus operation in nearby Brighton, had also been in the running.

Go-Ahead had more success at the other extremity of the South Coast, in Plymouth, where the council announced sale plans in the summer of 2009. This prompted rival city operator First to introduce new local services, in the realisation that it would be unlikely to be allowed to buy the company because of concerns that the group would then dominate the market. The company was bought by Go-Ahead in December.

Towards the end of 2009 Caerphilly Council decided to sell its Islwyn Borough Transport business. With just

### THE SURVIVING MUNICIPALS

- Blackpool Transport Services
- Cardiff Bus
- Halton Borough Transport
- Ipswich Buses
- Lothian Buses
- Newport Transport
- Nottingham City Transport
- Reading Transport
- Rossendale Transport
- Thamesdown Transport
- Warrington Borough Transport

42 buses, this was the smallest of Britain's 12 surviving municipal bus companies. It was bought by Stagecoach. Its sale left Halton, with 57 vehicles, as Britain's smallest municipal fleet. Lothian, with just over 700, remains the largest, followed by Nottingham (320).

There are now just 11 local-authority-owned bus fleets in Britain — at least in the sense in which the term is normally understood. There are in fact a small number of other local-authority bus operations, often focussed on some particular niche operation. Worcestershire County Council, for example, runs its own buses on park-and-ride services in Worcester, whilst Dumfries & Galloway Council has buses running on school services as well as on some regular routes. But one thing is for sure: the great days of municipally owned bus operation are gone. For ever.

**Blackburn Borough Transport was bought by Transdev in 2007 and was soon absorbed into Transdev's existing Lancashire United business, which served the town and the surrounding area. Here a 1999 Volvo B10BLE with Wright body leaves Blackburn bus station for neighbouring Accrington.**

**MISSING MUNICIPALS – who runs the services now?**

| | |
|---|---|
| **Barrow** | Stagecoach |
| **Blackburn** | Transdev |
| **Bournemouth** | Transdev |
| **Brighton** | Go-Ahead |
| **Burnley & Pendle** | Transdev |
| **Chester** | First |
| **Chesterfield** | Stagecoach |
| **Cleveland** | Stagecoach |
| **Colchester** | Arriva (TGM) |
| **Cynon Valley** | Stagecoach |
| **Darlington** | Arriva |
| **Derby** | Arriva |
| **Eastbourne** | Stagecoach |
| **Fylde** | Blackpool Transport |
| **Grampian** | First |
| **Great Yarmouth** | First |
| **Grimsby-Cleethorpes** | Stagecoach |
| **Hartlepool** | Stagecoach |
| **Hull** | Stagecoach |
| **Hyndburn** | Transdev |
| **Inter Valley Link** | Stagecoach |
| **Islwyn** | Stagecoach |
| **Lancaster** | Stagecoach |
| **Leicester** | First |
| **Lincoln** | Stagecoach |
| **Maidstone** | Arriva |
| **Merthyr Tydfil** | Stagecoach |
| **Northampton** | First |
| **Plymouth** | Go-Ahead |
| **Portsmouth** | First |
| **Preston** | Stagecoach |
| **Southampton** | First |
| **Southend** | Arriva |
| **Taff-Ely** | Stagecoach |
| **Tayside** | National Express |

# The twilight zone

Not all redundant buses and coaches head straight to the breaker's yard. **Tony Wilson** illustrates a selection of vehicles which found new and sometimes surprising roles in their twilight years.

***Left:*** **In the late 1970s a collaboration between London Transport and Obsolete Fleet provided the capital with some of the first open-toppers to run a full-time service around the major sights. Here an ex-Midland Red BMMO D9 trundles along the Embankment in May 1977, displaying prominent advertising for a well-known Scottish libation.**

***Below:*** **Purpose-built for motorway operation and formerly operated by Bournemouth-based Shamrock & Rambler, this MCW Metroliner, along with many others of its type, had by April 1990 been redeployed on tourist work in Central London. The roof had been removed and the top deck was able to provide around 60 seats for tourists to experience the sights and sounds of the capital.**

*Above:* **By now owned by neighbouring East Kent and dedicated to Seaspeed contract work, a former Maidstone & District Daimler Fleetline/Marshall saloon rests between duties at Dover Marine station in September 1978.**

*Below:* **New in 1969 to Gales of Haslemere, Surrey, this Plaxton-bodied Bedford VAL70 found itself 34 years later working a hard day's sightseeing on a Beatles-inspired Magical Mystery Tour of Liverpool, being seen in June 2003.**

*Above:* **All-over advertising has proved to be a useful source of revenue since the first appeared more than 40 years ago on a London Routemaster. However, in February 1974 the forecourt of the John Lyon public house in North Wembley was host to a much older promotional vehicle in the form of this ex-London Transport RT-type AEC Regent.**

*Below:* **In the 1980s many of London Transport's unloved Fleetlines saw further service with a wide range of users. In later years this example was extensively rebuilt for use as a hospitality vehicle and when photographed in Chesterfield in May 2002 had been painted to promote the VK alcoholic brand.**

***Above:*** **Many time-expired buses and coaches have proved useful as mobile or static homesteads. Noted near Gillingham, Norfolk, in the 1970s was this 1937 Leyland Tiger TS7 with 1950 Harrington body. Still in the livery of its original owner, Maidstone & District, it would survive to pass into preservation.**

***Right:*** **A former Ribble Leyland PD2/Burlingham at Epsom Downs on the occasion of the Derby in June 1976. It was by now owned by the Romany Guild, 'ACERT' – with its horse-racing connotations – being an acronym for the Advisory Council for the Education of Romany and other Travellers.**

*Left:* **New to Greater Glasgow PTE in 1974 as a conventional double-decker, this Alexander-bodied Leyland Atlantean came off worse in an encounter with a low bridge. Rebuilt by the PTE (by now renamed Strathclyde) as a single-decker, it served as the prototype for a number of similar conversions, the vehicles in question being used to replace hired Seddon Midis on the shuttle service which linked Glasgow's two main railway stations. This photograph was taken at Glasgow Central in August 1984.**

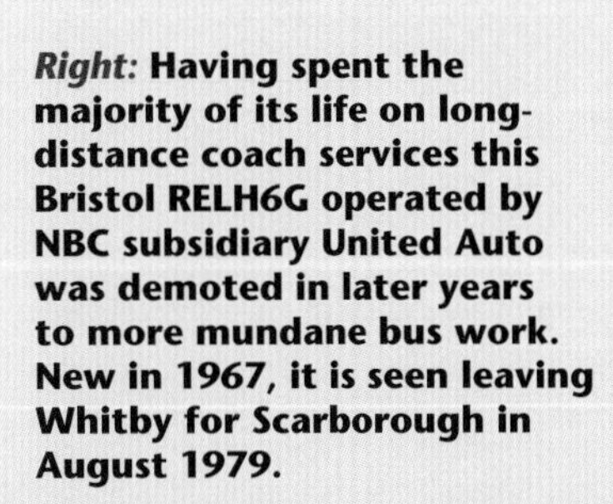

*Right:* **Having spent the majority of its life on long-distance coach services this Bristol RELH6G operated by NBC subsidiary United Auto was demoted in later years to more mundane bus work. New in 1967, it is seen leaving Whitby for Scarborough in August 1979.**

***Left:*** **Over the years many time-expired buses have been converted for further use as service vehicles. Pictured in Harrogate, this ECW-bodied Bristol K in the West Yorkshire fleet has had its roof removed, befitting its new role as a tree-lopper. The forward-entrance conversion prompts idle thoughts of what might have been …**

***Right:*** **Generally it is city-based buses that are relegated to less arduous work upon the completion of their initial years of toil, but such is not always the case. Having spent the majority of its career on rural work in the West Country, this ex-Western National Bristol LS5G was destined to end its days pounding around the concrete jungle of the Heathrow Airport complex on transfer work, being seen pulling away from Terminal 1 in May 1972.**

***Left:*** **Buses have been used extensively by the film and television industry, especially for on-location catering, little work being required to remove a few seats and install tables etc. In the 1970s Location Facilities of Feltham employed this former Wilts & Dorset Bristol KSW, displaying a seemingly enigmatic (but entirely genuine) W&D destination.**

# Deregulated? Well, yes ... and no

***Buses* editor Alan Millar looks at the controversial role the OFT has played in shaping Britain's bus industry.**

When we think about the Transport Act 1985 and the radical changes it brought to the British bus industry outside London, our thoughts usually start and finish with deregulation and privatisation.

Those were the big visible changes in the shape of the bus industry with which many of us grew up. The certainties of a regulated market for bus services, where it was nigh on impossible for newcomers to challenge established operators, came to an abrupt end. And the dominance of public ownership — state-owned company buses in town and country, local-government ownership in the big cities and many smaller cities and large towns — also ended fairly quickly, starting with the break-up and privatisation of the National Bus Company.

But the Act, and the July 1984 White Paper on Buses that preceded it, contained another measure that also upset the certainties of old, and continues to cause much friction between the industry and government today: the involvement of the competition authorities.

The White Paper, Conservative transport secretary Nicholas Ridley's manifesto for change on British bus services outside London, set out a vision in which competition would create a more efficient and innovative bus industry, requiring less public subsidy and charging lower fares. Breaking up NBC was a key to this, as privatisation of it intact could simply create a private-sector monopoly.

To make all this possible, restrictive-trade-practices legislation was extended to buses, operators being obliged to furnish the Director General of Fair Trading (DGFT) with details of any mutual agreements they reached, in order to establish whether these were in the public interest.

Soon the names of the Office of Fair Trading and the Monopolies & Mergers Commission became as familiar in bus circles as those of the traffic commissioners, the quasi-judicial regulators to whom the industry had been — and remained — answerable since 1931. In April 1999 the Competition Commission – with greater powers and penalties – took the place of the MMC.

The MMC had already had an impact on the public-sector bus industry by 1984, but hardly in a way that the competition regulators have since. It had investigated London Transport's bus-overhauling arrangements, providing the ammunition its management needed to replace the Chiswick and Aldenham central works with less-expensive facilities. And it carried out a benchmarking study of three NBC subsidiaries (Bristol, Cheltenham District and Trent), one municipal (Cardiff) and one PTE (West Midlands), which reached no startling conclusions.

Both of those reports betrayed an ability for lay people to be swayed by easily grasped issues that were not really at the heart of what the MMC was being asked to do, but which also captured the imagination of people interested in buses. The London report exposed the apparent gulf between what LT said was wrong with its Daimler and Leyland Fleetlines and the high regard in which these buses were held by those who took them off its hands. And the five-operator study was similarly obsessed by the high maintenance costs of the relatively few Leyland 501-engined Bristol VRs in some NBC fleets against those with Gardner 6LXBs.

A conspiracy theorist might wonder whether someone dangled the likes of the VR-engine issue before the MMC so it would not upset a more fundamental apple-cart in the way the industry worked. If so, the post-1985 changes soon exposed the industry to a level of scrutiny far beyond matters of obsolete Leyland powerplants. They also exposed it to people with little knowledge of how the bus industry got to where it was in 1986, and who had no need to care about it either. The OFT and MMC were charged with making competition work.

### A predisposition to consolidation

The trouble is that the bus industry got to where it was in 1986 by doing a lot of things that conflicted with a remit of achieving pure, open and equal competition. Read the histories of any major operator and there is usually a similar tale to be told — of a business driving smaller competitors off the road and/or buying them up, of major shareholders (usually big groups and main-line railways, later the state and local government) providing the capital to grow bigger and stronger, of area agreements with other operators to dominate an area without competing, and of jointly operated routes and inter-available tickets.

Rightly or wrongly, the received bus-industry view was that these arrangements benefited passengers as well as operators. Competition for the same passengers on the same routes was widely perceived — and portrayed — as 'wasteful'. Co-ordination, of different operators' bus services and of bus and rail services, was A Good Thing that held the possibility of making public transport almost as seamless to use as jumping in one's own car, turning the key and taking it wherever one chose.

Even with a new generation of younger managers steering their businesses in new more commercially focussed directions from 1986, the urge to consolidate, dominate and not compete wastefully remained irresistible — not least in the way that the patchwork of briefly independent ex-NBC companies began to be stitched back together in new private-sector groups.

When they were being privatised, adjoining businesses — 'contiguous' was the word used at the time — could not be sold to the same owner, and a couple of deals were halted when buyers were found to have set up nominally separate companies to buy neighbouring NBC subsidiaries. Yet the 1980s were not over when the emerging new groups began buying ex-NBC companies and linking some of them into new regional giants – proof either that bus-industry economics demand such scale or that 60 or 70 years of consolidation predisposed it to mergers and regional dominance.

The ingredients were sufficient to ensure a steady series of confrontations between the industry and the OFT and MMC. Pivotal to many of these were the authorities' belief that bus operators should compete with one another for a discrete market of bus travellers, and the operators' argument that buses actually compete in a wider travel market, primarily the private car but also taxis and, to an extent, trains. That difference of opinion is as stark as I write this in 2010 as it was more than 20 years ago.

Early on there were several complaints to the OFT from smaller operators alleging unfair competition from bigger fleets. These usually centred on the numbers of vehicles the

**In 1981, five years before all British bus services outside London were deregulated, Hereford & Worcester County Council took advantage of powers in the Transport Act 1980 to conduct a deregulation trial on city and rural services in and around Hereford, where the dominant operator was NBC's Midland Red subsidiary. Among the operators taking advantage of this first opportunity in 50 years to compete was Primrose Motors, one of whose Plaxton Elite-bodied coaches is seen waiting behind a Midland Red Leyland Leopard and Leyland National in a street with parking restrictions and narrow pavements packed with waiting passengers.** AUTHOR'S COLLECTION

big operators were running, coupled with the fact that these were scheduled directly ahead of their own and that the big operators' fares were uneconomically low. Two features characterised the OFT's handling of such complaints, one being that investigating them took so long that the smaller operator had already given up, sold out or gone bust long before there was an official report, the other that the OFT mostly found in favour of the larger operator.

One of the OFT's first pronouncements to have an impact on the industry was its judgement that jointly operated services were potentially anti-competitive. In the era of regulation joint operation appeared to make great operational sense. If operators at either end of a longer route ran it from each end, they could offer early departures and late arrivals from the extremities without having to run a lot of dead mileage to achieve it. And in any case the joint operators were often in common ownership, subsidiaries of one of the state-owned groups.

Some such services became jointly operated when the groups split larger subsidiaries into smaller ones, for example when the Scottish Bus Group carved Alexander's in three in 1961 and the Glasgow–Dundee route became a joint operation between Alexander (Midland) and Alexander (Northern), and various routes between Glasgow and Fife became joint Midland and Alexander (Fife) services.

The OFT viewed joint operation as akin to a cartel shutting other businesses out of the market, and insisted that such arrangements should be cleared with it before permitting them to continue. Its quest to outlaw cartels also saw operators reported to the Restrictive Practices Court when suspected of meeting secretly to fix fares, routes or tender prices, and operators became increasingly wary of discussing matters of mutual financial interest for fear of incurring the OFT's wrath.

## Bristol and Portsmouth — a tale of two cities

One of the first OFT/MMC merger inquiries followed the amalgamation in 1988 of Badgerline Holdings and Midland Red West Holdings. The merger was typical of the rapidly changing structure of the bus industry.

In September 1983 NBC had split the Bristol Omnibus Co into two smaller operations as part of an ongoing process throughout its Southern Region; this was done for administrative reasons, before privatisation was on the Government's agenda. Bristol retained control of routes in an around Bristol itself, Bath, Wells and Weston-super-Mare, whilst services in the Cheltenham,

**Stagecoach had begun amalgamating Portsmouth CityBus and Southdown services before it was ordered to sell the business. Here a Southdown-liveried Leyland National with Portsmouth Transit fleetnames precedes a competing example in the People's Provincial fleet. In First ownership Portsmouth Transit and Provincial would be merged into one without incurring the wrath of the competition authorities.** ALAN MILLAR

**Following Nicholas Ridley's instruction that Stagecoach sell Portsmouth CityBus, two ex-CityBus Alexander-bodied Leyland Atlanteans pass each other in the early stages of Transit Holdings ownership. Still in CityBus red and cream, they have Portsmouth Transit fleetnames.** ALAN MILLAR

Gloucester, Stroud and Swindon areas passed to a new company, the Cheltenham & Gloucester Omnibus Co. Subsequently, in 1985, the Bristol company's operations were further divided, into City Line, operating Bristol city services, and Badgerline, responsible for all other routes in Avon and north Somerset.

Badgerline and Cheltenham & Gloucester were the subject of two of the first management buy-outs, in 1986, while City Line remained with NBC for a further year before being acquired by Midland Red West, another of the early buy-outs. The merger of Badgerline and Midland Red West thus reunited two of the three parts of the Bristol Omnibus Co, and the OFT was sufficiently concerned to refer the matter to the MMC.

The six-member MMC panel that reported back in 1989 was divided on the issue, deciding by a majority of four to two that the merger 'may be expected' to be against the public interest. It accepted, however, that the merger also brought benefits and confined its objection to the market for tendered services, asking the DGFT to demand undertakings from Badgerline over its future behaviour when competing for tendered work.

If the industry imagined this set the pattern for all future investigations, any complacency was swept away a year later, in 1990, with the first of several confrontations with Stagecoach, which also had been busy buying up ex-NBC companies from debt-burdened managers and acquiring some of their competitors. Among its strategic purchases in 1989 was Southdown, to which it added — among other businesses — Portsmouth CityBus, the former municipal undertaking. The Portsmouth purchase gave Stagecoach similar dominance of that city to Badgerline's in Bristol, and the MMC concluded not only that there were benefits to be gained from the merger but also that an order to sell it off would 'bring considerable dislocation of services and detriment to passengers'.

The MMC, however, could only advise. The final say on such decisions rested with the Department of Trade & Industry, whose secretary of state — following the usual merry-go-round of Government ministers — was none

**An SUT Leyland National and South Yorkshire Transport MCW Metrobus in central Sheffield.** PHIL HALEWOOD

**An ECW-bodied Bristol LH6L in Stockton, painted in the Caldaire version of Trimdon Motor Services blue and cream livery. The bus had been new to Bristol Omnibus in 1978.** ALAN MILLAR

other than Nicholas Ridley. In what turned out to be his last act in the bus arena before resigning from the Government over an unassociated indiscreet remark, he over-ruled the MMC and ordered the OFT to have Stagecoach divest itself of its Portsmouth business and sell it to someone else in order to restore competition.

Stagecoach, which rarely accepted such interventions without pursuing the case to higher authority (or at least without expressing its feelings in public), eventually complied and in January 1991 sold the bulk of its Portsmouth operations to Harry Blundred's Transit Holdings, a business which, following some initial skirmishing in Transit's heartland of Torquay, it now saw as a friendly rival. It would later buy Transit's operations in Devon and Oxford, after Blundred had sold the Portsmouth operation on to FirstGroup.

## The courts get involved

The threat of divestment began to spead far and wide. South Yorkshire Transport, still in the public sector as an arms'-length ex-PTE company, had bought up several new-start independents in Sheffield and amalgamated them into an enlarged version of one of them, SUT, to create a low-cost subsidiary. Following a less favourable MMC report than Stagecoach had attracted in Portsmouth, Peter Lilley — Ridley's successor at the DTI — ordered it to sell this 120-vehicle business in 1990.

Lilley took a tougher line a couple of months later when the MMC reported on Caldaire Holdings' acquisition of Trimdon Motor Services. Caldaire owned United Automobile, and Trimdon had been among the biggest pre-deregulation independents serving the same parts of County Durham as United. The MMC seemed prepared to nail some conditions to Caldaire's mast, requiring it to accept restrictions relating to its fares and service frequencies, but the minister wanted more: the OFT should consider getting Caldaire to sell part of the combined business.

Neither of these divestments happened, but there was a lengthy legal process before the Government backed down. SYT appealed to the High Court, which found in its favour, concluding that the MMC had exceeded its powers in ordering the sale of SUT, and stating that Sheffield was too small an area and not 'significant' in the context of the entire country. Lilley and the MMC then took the case to the Court of Appeal, lost out when it ruled against them in November 1991, but then won the argument a year later in the House of Lords, then the highest court in the land.

The SYT case cast doubt over the validity of the order for Caldaire to sell routes, although the group agreed a plan with the OFT to sell seven buses' worth of work if its own application for a judicial review came to nothing. Viewed from a wider perspective, seven buses' worth of semi-rural operation hardly seemed worth such high principle.

In the end, with Michael Heseltine now in charge at the DTI, the Government relented during 1993, backing down from requiring either SYT or Westcourt (which by now owned Caldaire's operations in North East England) to sell anything and instead settling for some behavioural undertakings.

Matters took a different turn elsewhere in 1993 when, following complaints from three smaller operators about predatory pricing, blocking of bus stops and a refusal to let them use its Pentagon bus station in Chatham, management-owned Maidstone & District was referred by the OFT to the MMC. The latter found against M&D, imposing conditions on fares and service levels and an obligation to make space in the bus station for other operators.

Such was his unhappiness over the judgement that M&D Operations Director Roger Davies, one of the co-owners of the business, left the company, saying that the MMC had made it impossible to undertake his job effectively. Ironically, around a year later the OFT cleared M&D's acquisition of Bygone Buses, one of the companies that complained about its behaviour, without reference to the MMC.

## Stagecoach riles the regulators

Stagecoach was starting to find itself more in the regulators' sights than most of the other operators, perhaps because it was prepared to push a point farther to see how far the authorities would bend or just because it acquired more companies.

During 1993 Lancaster City Transport had come on the market, and, as the other dominant operator in the area, Stagecoach had most to gain from making the acquisition. But, as the Portsmouth case already had shown, that could be reason enough for the MMC to get involved and for a sympathetic Government minister to rule against it.

Stagecoach therefore expanded its operations ahead of the sale, registering its own routes over those of LCT and precipitating a deal that saw it buy the LCT depot and a few of its buses, but not the business itself. However, you mess with regulators at your peril, and the MMC considered this was still a merger and, more to the point, one that might be expected to act against the public interest.

Just as it had done with M&D, the MMC imposed strict conditions. In particular, if Stagecoach registered new services or cut fares to see off a competitor, it had to maintain these for three years after the competitor withdrew. And if it refused to abide by these terms, it would be compelled to sell the LCT depot.

Undaunted, Stagecoach chanced its arm even more audaciously with the competition police in November 1994 when it stormed into Darlington. Here the conditions were different, as United Auto, the town's other dominant operator, was effectively precluded from making a bid to buy Darlington Transport from the borough council.

Stagecoach had begun buying up the former municipal and PTE undertakings in North East England and duly bid for Darlington. So too did Badgerline and Traction Group. Traction Group bid highest and looked set to buy, but the Darlington workforce was unhappy, especially as it was suggested that Traction was merely a stalking horse for a sale that would eventually see Darlington Transport amalgamated with United.

Stagecoach claimed it was invited to register routes in competition, which it did. Traction promptly withdrew its bid, Stagecoach recruited most of Darlington Transport's drivers, and the municipal company imploded and went into administration. Stagecoach had been running buses free until its registrations took effect and bought the depot from the administrator, selling it for redevelopment.

**An Alexander Dash-bodied Dennis Dart of Arriva North East branded for a Darlington town service. This was among the vehicles that Stagecoach sold to Arriva in 2007 when it pulled out of Darlington. It was new to Stagecoach's now sold business in London.** GARY MITCHELHILL

**Having sold the United Counties depot at Huntingdon in 1997 to stave off an MMC referral, Stagecoach reacquired it 11 years later as part of Cavalier Contracts. During the intervening period Blazefield owned the Huntingdon operation, rebranding it as Huntingdon & District and applying this livery from its Sovereign fleet in Hertfordshire. Cavalier later adopted this as its livery, seen on a UVG UrbanStar-bodied Dennis Dart SLF in Peterborough in 2009, with Stagecoach fleet numbers and legal lettering.** ALAN MILLAR

The MMC was called in to investigate what *Buses* Editor Stephen Morris described at the time as 'a gross act of piracy'. When it reported back the following year the MMC described Stagecoach's behaviour as 'predatory, deplorable and against the public interest' and slapped on conditions similar to those required of the company in Lancaster and of M&D in the Medway Towns. Stagecoach Chief Executive Brian Souter was in any case soon regretting the deal, admitting to transport journalist and author Christian Wolmar that 'PR damage far and away offset any benefit that the deal brought us'.

In 2007 Stagecoach sought — and obtained — OFT approval to sell the Darlington operation to Arriva, which by then owned what had been United and thus became the only operator of commercial services in Darlington.

## Mainline and Strathclyde

Stagecoach attracted the attention of another strand of MMC scrutiny when it bought shareholdings of around 20% in two former PTE companies now owned by their respective employees — Mainline, as SYT had become, and SB Holdings, which owned Strathclyde Buses (and Kelvin Central). Both deals were seen as a step towards eventual 100% ownership by Stagecoach.

When it ruled on the Mainline purchase in 1995 the MMC recommended that Stagecoach's shareholding be limited to 20%, ensuring that Mainline retained its access to Stagecoach finance but reducing the perception of it as one of the group's subsidiaries. Once again a Government minister thought the MMC had not gone far enough, Consumer Affairs minister Jonathan Evans instructing Stagecoach to sell its shares and requiring Brian Souter to relinquish his seat on the Mainline board. Stagecoach challenged the ruling, but before the courts got a chance to consider it Mainline struck a deal with FirstBus — newly created by the merger of Badgerline and GRT — for it to acquire the 20%, apparently unchallenged by the MMC or Government ministers.

Shortly afterwards Evans issued a similar ruling with regard to SB Holdings, though this time the MMC held the same view, arguing that the shareholding could be expected to operate against the public interest. The MMC had also conducted a parallel investigation into SB Holdings' acquisition of Kelvin Central, a former Scottish Bus Group subsidiary, which increased SB's share of the local bus market from 43% to 66%, but both the MMC and Evans allowed this to stand, as there had been little competition between the two operators immediately before the takeover.

Stagecoach eventually reached an out-of-court settlement with the DTI which allowed it to bid for either company should they be offered for sale, but by then it was too late, and First bought the remaining 80% of Mainline in 1998.

Neither Government nor MMC was done with Glasgow. In May 1996 First agreed a deal to buy all of SB Holdings, including Stagecoach's shareholding. Added to what it already owned in Scotland, this gave First contiguous services from the border with England at Berwick up to and across much of the populous central belt.

First had restructured its other central Scottish operations, splitting Edinburgh-based SMT in two, with depots shared between its Midland Bluebird and Lowland subsidiaries. Perhaps it soon wished that it had left them alone, for the MMC persuaded the new Consumer Affairs minister, John Taylor, that the SB Holdings takeover was against the public interest.

Taylor gave First two options: sell SB Holdings in its entirety or sell one of its Glasgow depots and the entire enlarged Midland Bluebird. This was early 1997. Perhaps signalling its continuing interest in Glasgow, Stagecoach launched competitive new services there in late April, around a week before a general election saw the Conservatives swept from power after 18 years. First hit back by competing with Stagecoach in Fife and Ayrshire.

First's post-election lobbying persuaded Margaret Beckett, Labour's first Trade & Industry secretary, to let things be. Because of Stagecoach's expansion in Glasgow the MMC felt that the divestment requirement should be reduced, but the new minister went farther: First could keep the lot, provided it agreed to be bound by behavioural undertakings.

## Selling to avoid a referral

In the meantime Stagecoach had been obliged to give more ground, in 1996, six months after it acquired management-owned Cambus Holdings, which owned Cambus and Viscount in Cambridgeshire and MK Metro in Milton Keynes. In NBC days the Milton Keynes business had been part of United Counties, and Stagecoach had owned the remaining north Bedfordshire and Northamptonshire part of United Counties since NBC sold it in 1987.

Worried about Stagecoach's dominance, the OFT hatched a plan for Stagecoach to sell United Counties' Bedford and Biggleswade depots, which happened to be the company's best commercial performers. Stagecoach instead persuaded the OFT to let it sell Huntingdon, then the weakest commercial performer, and MK Metro, which was a loss-making nightmare. Thus was a deal done that satisfied operator and regulator without calling in the hawks at the MMC.

Stagecoach was told to find one buyer to take both and in 1997 struck a bargain with industry entrepreneur Julian Peddle, who rebranded the Huntingdon business as Premier Buses. He sold that operation on in 1998 to Blazefield, which later sold it to Cavalier Contracts, which sold it in 2008 to, of all people, Stagecoach. The OFT investigated and cleared that deal.

Peddle sold MK Metro to Arriva, which following OFT clearance merged it into its Shires & Essex business, which includes the south Bedfordshire and Hertfordshire operations of NBC's United Counties.

Not that Arriva has escaped the attention of the regulators. In 1998 the MMC ordered it to sell Lutonian Buses, a long-established minibus operator it had acquired after a competitive battle. It seemed that Arriva's own Challenger business, set up to compete with Lutonian, had used aggressive tactics that forced Lutonian to sell; such action is frowned upon by the regulators and has repeatedly

**Glenvale adopted a GTL identity and the same red and cream livery that Arriva removed speedily from the MTL North fleet in Liverpool. It also operated a large fleet of vehicles well past their youth, like this ex-London MCW Metrobus.** ALEX HORNBY

**A 15m Plaxton Panther-bodied Volvo B12BT of Park's of Hamilton, in its livery of Citylink blue and yellow with Park's fleetnames.** RICHARD WALTER

prompted them to act. Arriva took until September 2000 to sell Lutonian to a consortium involving Julian Peddle and the owner of Aylesbury independent Red Rose.

After acquiring employee-owned MTL North, the former PTE bus company on Merseyside, in 2000 and adding it to its former NBC operations in the area, Arriva was presented with another divestment ultimatum: either sell its 130-vehicle Gillmoss depot in Liverpool and the routes it operated, or face a Competition Commission reference. Go-Ahead emerged as the preferred bidder out of four short-listed in 2001 but pulled out to concentrate on bus, rail and airport-handling expansion opportunities in South East England. Instead Gillmoss depot went to Glenvale Transport, a company set up by former MTL managers who also retained the old MTL livery but with a GTL fleetname. Arriva was prevented from competing against Glenvale for three years. Glenvale acquired CMT Buses, one of the other companies that had short-listed to buy Gillmoss, in 2003 and sold out to Stagecoach in July 2005.

## The curious question of buses, coaches and trains

One slightly bizarre aspect of the involvement of the competition authorities has been their treatment of the bus and rail markets. Indeed, some would question why they are involved at all in the highly regulated railway business.

Bus groups have bid for and won rail franchises from what today is the Department for Transport since the railways began to be privatised in 1993, and Stagecoach and National Express were among the first to take mainstream rail operations back into private ownership.

Despite being scrutinised closely by transport civil servants and cleared by ministers, rail franchise awards also were referred to the OFT and occasionally to the MMC. So it was that in 1997 Margaret Beckett referred National Express's acquisition of the ScotRail franchise to the MMC, as NatEx already owned Scottish Citylink Coaches. The OFT was prepared to let NatEx off a reference to the MMC if it was prepared to sell Citylink, but the minister thought otherwise and also got the MMC to investigate NatEx's award of the Central Trains franchise.

The MMC passed the Central Trains acquisition but recommended that NatEx be ordered to sell Citylink, stating that the merger could act against the public interest on routes where Citylink and ScotRail ran parallel services, notably Glasgow–Edinburgh and Glasgow/Edinburgh–Aberdeen/Inverness. Beckett agreed, and the following year NatEx sold Citylink to Metroline, a London bus contractor with no interests elsewhere in Britain.

Clearly the MMC considered then that coaches and trains competed to carry the same passengers. So did one of Beckett's successors, Stephen Byers, when he conditionally approved NatEx's acquisition of the Prism Rail business, whose franchises included operation of trains between Stansted Airport and London. A price of Government approval of that takeover was that NatEx should undertake to the OFT not to reduce parallel coach services or raise coach fares above the level it charged between London and Heathrow.

The authorities' perception of coach and train markets had changed by 2005, when Stagecoach and Scottish Citylink entered into a new joint venture (35% owned by Stagecoach) that ended 13 months of head-to-head competition on the same routes where, seven years earlier, the MMC was convinced that Citylink and ScotRail competed. Singapore-based ComfortDelGro had by then acquired Metroline and Citylink, and NatEx had lost the rail franchise to First.

A sign of a changing attitude to bus and rail travel, for those who chose to read it, came early in 2006 when the Competition Commission cleared First's award of the Greater Western rail franchise, serving many places in the West Country and South Wales in which First also operated buses. 'In most of the areas we have looked at, bus and train services have different characteristics, and the passengers using them have different requirements,' said Diana Guy, who chaired the inquiry group. 'Even in those areas where there was some potential for competition, we found the profit incentive was very small for an operator of both bus and train services to take advantage of its position to shift passengers from bus to rail by raising fares or altering services.'

Within eight years the competition regulators had changed from seeing surface public transport as one market to regarding it as one in which bus and train passengers were largely different people. That view prevailed when the OFT and Competition Commission investigated the Stagecoach/Citylink joint venture, a view perhaps given added force by the fact that Stagecoach and ComfortDelGro had concluded the deal without informing the OFT beforehand.

When it published its final report in October 2006 the Competition Commission pulled no punches. 'Customers benefit from competition, and we do not see how this joint venture can preserve these benefits for passengers when previously these companies had been competing vigorously

**A Preston Bus Leyland Lynx in March 2009, still in its former owner's full livery but with Stagecoach fleetname. Although Preston's few Lynxes were taken out of service soon afterwards, the Competition Commission forbade their sale.** STEVEN J. ALLEN

**The message displayed on the front of this ex-Preston Bus East Lancs Esteem-bodied Scania N94UB seems prophetic. It was among a handful of vehicles painted before the OFT's inquiry called a halt to such symbols of integration.** STEVEN J. ALLEN

for their custom,' said Chairman John Baillie. 'Other forms of transport act as only weak constraints, if any, on coach fares. Rail fares are generally too high in comparison to act as a constraint, and there was insufficient evidence to persuade us that the car was a constraint.'

The report stated that either the joint venture should be broken up (which would have restored a level of competition in which both parties at best broke even and probably were losing money) or that some of its services should be sold to another party independent of the joint venture.

Under the previous regime, with the MMC, the final decision on such matters rested with a Government minister, which (as past experience showed) could sometimes lead to even more drastic remedies than the competition watchdogs recommended. But that had changed after the Competition Commission was established in 1999, the Government having decided that, other than where national security was at risk, the commission would advise and implement on its own.

The Citylink case had an added dimension, as the Scottish Parliament became responsible for transport (including awarding the ScotRail franchise) from its formation in 1999, while competition legislation was a matter, in the jargon of devolution, 'reserved' to Westminster.

Political lobbying and all-party complaints cut no ice, and the joint venture eventually accepted the commission's judgement and concluded a sale which suggested that the competition authorities were keener on something being seen to be done than something that actually restored full-scale competition. Some journeys on Aberdeen/Inverness–Glasgow/Edinburgh services — known as 'Saltire Cross' routes because their interconnecting northeast-to-west and north-to-east paths resemble the Scottish flag — were sold in February 2008 to Park's of Hamilton, which was already a contractor to the joint venture. Its coaches remained in Citylink colours but with Park's fleetnames instead of Citylink's. Log on to its website to book travel on its services and you will be directed to the Citylink site, which shows which departures are Park's and which are the joint venture's.

## Preston, Cardiff and the two-year inquiry

By now the seeds of another Stagecoach confrontation were being sown. The group wanted to buy Preston Bus, the only ex-municipal operator still owned by its employees, but its offer was rebuffed. It registered new routes in the city in direct competition from July 2007, prompting Preston Bus to increase its services and lease new buses.

By the end of 2008 Preston Bus had been badly weakened and could no longer survive as an independent business. Arriva was prepared to buy it, but only if it could

***Above:* An Eastbourne Buses MAN 14.220 with MCV Evolution body, one of the newest vehicles taken over by Stagecoach.** MARK LYONS

***Left:* Cavendish competed with Eastbourne Buses until Stagecoach bought both companies. Its fleet consisted mainly of Plaxton Pointer-bodied Dennis Dart SLFs, many of them in this livery influenced by the traditional Southdown look.** BEN MORROLL

also acquire the Stagecoach (Ribble) depot in the city. For Preston Bus the best answer was the deal it had rejected around two years earlier, and it duly sold out to Stagecoach in January 2009.

Stagecoach rapidly rationalised the networks into one and began repainting buses in its corporate livery, but the OFT — perhaps more annoyed by Stagecoach's tactics before the takeover than by the takeover itself — referred the matter to the Competition Commission, which reported back before the end of the year with the uncompromising message that the merger be undone and Preston Bus, or Preston operations of equivalent size, be sold to restore competition in the city.

As with all such investigations, it cast a blight of sorts at Preston while it was being carried out. Repainting of the fleet was halted, and measures were put in place to manage it separately from Stagecoach's other services in North West England.

**2 Travel and Cardiff Bus competing. The OFT's decision to refer the local-bus market to the Competition Commission in 2010 was influenced partly by this battle in the Welsh capital, where Cardiff Bus used plain-white Optare MetroRiders to compete against aged 2 Travel single-deckers like this Alexander Dash-bodied Volvo B6, which was new to Stagecoach.** JOHN CALLOW

A few weeks either side of the Preston takeover Stagecoach had bought Eastbourne Buses, from the local council, and Cavendish Motor Services, its main competitor. Those deals were also referred to the Competition Commission, which for a time looked likely to order its break-up. Indeed, that was its preliminary finding, but it later relented, acknowledging that Cavendish could not have survived in the manner it remained convinced that Preston Bus could.

As I write this, Stagecoach is appealing against the Preston ruling. However, the industry as a whole faces far wider and deeper Competition Commission scrutiny following the OFT's announcement in January 2010 that the commission will study bus operations across England outside London, Wales and Scotland in a two-year inquiry into its competitive activity. One of the triggers for this came in November 2008, when the OFT published a report into a two-year competitive battle between council-owned Cardiff Bus and 2 Travel Group, a small City-listed operator, on some of its busiest routes. The OFT concluded that Cardiff Bus had engaged in predatory conduct to eliminate 2 Travel, which collapsed in 2005.

The OFT carried out its own market study of local bus services during 2009, concluding that the London tendering system delivered fair competition and, rather more surprisingly, that the virtual monopoly enjoyed by state-owned Translink in Northern Ireland posed no competition concerns. But it remained concerned elsewhere by activities such as those it had condemned in Cardiff, as well as evidence that major operators might be manipulating the concessionary-travel budgets and restricting competition for tendered services.

What the two-year Competition Commission will recommend is anyone's guess at this stage. If its recommendations are radical the Government of 2012 will need to determine what new legislation is required — a process complicated by the need for devolved administrations in Edinburgh (which has powers to legislate for Scotland) and Cardiff (which has the option for Wales to adopt part or all of English legislation) to make their decisions.

The recommended changes could indeed be radical, for the OFT has been talking of the need for more competition in the market, but less on the streets. That implies a move to London-style quality contracts, already favoured by the six Passenger Transport Executives in England, but something that the Conservatives in Westminster have been resisting.

It would be an ironic twist of events if regulators brought into the bus industry to police deregulation in 1986 were to be the authors of its end a quarter of a century later.

***Above:*** **To the surprise of many the OFT pronounced itself happy with the bus market in Northern Ireland, where state-owned Translink's Metro and Ulsterbus subsidiaries have a near-monopoly of services. Here a Wright Renown-bodied Volvo B10BLE leads a line of Metro vehicles away from the imposing Belfast City Hall.** ALAN MILLAR

***Below:*** **Go North East and Arriva have been competing on routes north from Newcastle, where Go North East introduced its cut-price Bargain Bus service with older vehicles like this Alexander RH-bodied Leyland Olympian, new to Dublin Bus. Early in 2010 the OFT cleared a proposal by the two operators whereby Arriva would acquire Go North East's Ashington depot in exchange for its own depot at Hexham.** ALAN MILLAR

# Maltese mixture

Malta has long been a fascinating destination for anyone with an interest in buses, mixing as it does old and modern designs. All that could soon change under new Government plans. **John Young** paid the island a visit, and illustrates the current scene.

***Above:*** **There are around 30 ex-London Transport AEC Swifts in the route-bus fleet, although the degree of rebuilding and alteration varies significantly between vehicles. This one, originally LT's SMS200, dates back to 1971 and has a Marshall body. It is seen in Sliema amidst Festa decorations.**

***Right:*** **This ex-London Metro-Cammell-bodied Swift — it started life as LT's SMS603 — is considerably rebuilt since its days in Britain. The location is the layover area at Golden Bay terminus.**

*Above:* **Mellieha, on the main route to the Gozo ferry, is a pleasant village where the steep streets and coastal views offer much for the photographer. This is a Park Royal-bodied former London Swift, new in 1970 as SMS258, now with a touch of the Plaxton Paramount III about the front lower panel.**

*Below:* **Along with London's AEC Swifts, some AEC Reliance chassis from UK operators ended up in Malta and were rebodied locally. Illustrating the point at Valletta bus station, hub of the network, is this Spiteri-bodied bus which was new to North Western in 1963, at which time it had a Willowbrook body.**

***Right:*** **There are a dozen Bristol LHs in Malta, all bar one with ECW bus bodywork. This 1976 bus is one of three that were new to Crosville, and is seen (complete with Leyland Tiger Cub badge) in Bugibba on the main service to Valletta.**

***Below right:*** **Unique is this Ford Cargo with attractive locally-built Ramco body, passing through a deserted Birkirkara during siesta time on the service from Golden Bay to Valletta.**

***Below:*** **There cannot be many ex-London low-floor buses in service outside Britain. This is one of three Dennis Lances that were new to London Buses in 1994 and were among the first low-floor buses in the capital. More recently with the failed UK North operation in Manchester, it is seen at Bugibba bus station. The single-piece entrance door was a feature of early Wright-bodied low-floor buses.**

*Right:* **The Albion Clydesdale was a popular export model in the 1960s and 1970s. This one has a Brincat body and must be among very few Albion buses still in regular daily service. It is operating on the longest route on the island, from Valletta via Mosta, St Paul's Bay and Mellieha to Cirkewwa, from where the ferry to Gozo departs. This is Ghadira Bay.**

*Below:* **Typical of an earlier generation of flamboyant Maltese buses is this AEC Mercury dating from 1956, with bodywork by Farrugia. All buses from Valletta leave by way of Floriana, the location for this shot.**

*Right:* **The Leyland Lynx can be found in small numbers, examples originating from both the West Midlands and Preston Bus fleets. Heading through St Paul's Bay for Cirkewwa ferry is a former Preston bus, new in 1989.**

*Below:* **There are also a few Leyland Leopards in Malta. This smart Marshall-bodied PSU4 was new to Yorkshire Traction in 1968.**

*Right:* **This Plaxton Derwent-bodied Leopard PSU4 started life in 1976 with the West Yorkshire PTE. It is seen passing through Floriana, pursued by what might look like a Bristol LH but is in fact an ex-Blackburn Tiger Cub with an ECW front panel grafted onto its East Lancs body.**

*Above:* **Recent arrivals from the UK are a pair of ex-Stagecoach Yorkshire Volvo B6s with Alexander bodywork. This bus was new in 1995 to Nottingham City Transport and is seen at St Julian's Bay with the island's only skyscraper in the background.**

*Below:* **Bugibba is the location for this view of a smartly turned-out Bedford YRQ/Duple Dominant, one of a large number of former UK coaches in Malta. Most now have bus seats and have had large opening windows fitted.**

***Above:*** **Sporting both Bedford and Leyland Tiger Cub badges, this bus in Senglea Square might look like an early Bedford SB but is in fact a Dodge with Casha body.**

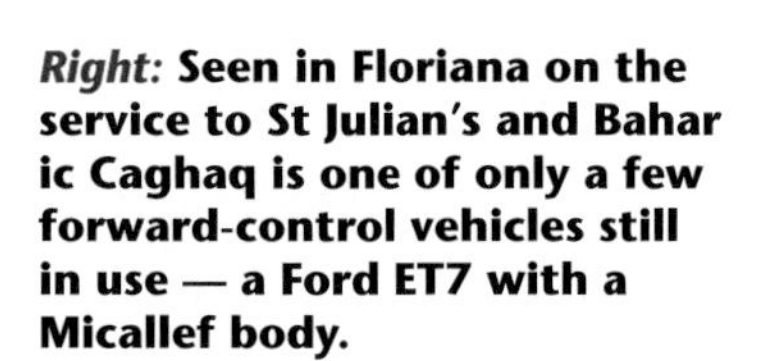

***Right:*** **Seen in Floriana on the service to St Julian's and Bahar ic Caghaq is one of only a few forward-control vehicles still in use — a Ford ET7 with a Micallef body.**

***Right:*** **Ghadira Bay, popular for its large expanse of sandy beach, is well served by bus. Picking up there is a rather different Ford, an R1014 with Duple Dominant bus body, which started life in 1978 as a Ford demonstrator.**

***Above:*** **One of the oldest (albeit much rebuilt) buses in Malta is this magnificent Willys Six Model 265 dating from 1934 with a Brincat body from 1949. Here it loads at St Paul's Bay, on the coast road to Sliema.**

***Left:*** **This ex-First Manchester Volvo Citybus is one of three of the type employed on sightseeing work and is seen passing through St Julian's Bay. It has an Alexander body and started life with Strathclyde Buses in 1989.**

# Municipal pride, Southern style

**Michael H. C. Baker** looks back at municipal buses on the Sussex coast.

*All photos by the author or from the author's collection.*

The days of towns' and cities' providing a wealth of facilities for their citizens, ranging from education, drainage, rat-catchers and so forth to public transport, gas and electricity belong to the past, although not all have been abandoned. It was an era of aldermen — large, dignified (not to say pompous) men sporting three-piece suits, gold watches and prominent chains. Men who were benevolent, perhaps, patronising too, who liked nothing better than to have their names inscribed for all eternity on a plaque commemorating the opening of the public baths, an extension to the town hall, or the tram depot.

A key figure, around whom the business of local administration revolved, was the Town Clerk. In my home town, Croydon, this post was held by one E. G. Taberner. His name appeared on the signs forbidding cycling on public footpaths, or ball games on the less-than-pristine patches of grass surrounding council housing estates, on letters from the town hall and much else of municipal import. It seemed to me he must be a very important person, although my impression of clerks generally was that they occupied fairly humble positions and were rather put-upon folk. In fact, unlike aldermen and tram inspectors, town clerks still exist; indeed, they are perhaps among the most important people in local government.

One group for whom they were responsible and one with whom the citizens came into daily contact, probably more often than any other, were the drivers, conductors

**Trolleybuses were operated by Brighton Corporation from 1939 to 1961. The initial fleet comprised 44 Weymann-bodied AECs, one of which is seen in the Old Steine alongside one of the trams it was replacing.**

**Brighton Hove & District's AEC Regents were older than those of the Corporation. Those who are familiar with Brighton may have trouble locating this view with an impressive ecclesiastical building as a backdrop. The building is in fact Bath Abbey — this wartime photo shows a BH&D Regent on hire to Bath Tramways. It had been new in 1931 and had a 52-seat Tilling body.**

and inspectors of trams and buses. Croydon Corporation operated a network of tram routes but never buses, for it was absorbed by London Transport in 1933, which was a bit before my time. However, its newest tramcars, virtually identical to London County Council's 'E1s', survived until the end of the first generation of trams in Croydon, in 1951.

The celebration of anniversaries was a good deal less in vogue 50 years ago than it has been of late, and my first sight of a vehicle decked out in full Croydon Corporation livery was in 1983, when 50 years of London Transport and 100 years of Croydon as a borough were marked in all sorts of interesting ways. Not the least of these was an LT Fleetline of Croydon garage repainted in the chocolate and off-white livery of Croydon Corporation, complete with the number 100 and 'CROYDON CORPORATION TRAMWAYS' emblazoned on the side.

Most Croydonians' favourite seaside resort was Brighton. Brighton has always been a town (now a city) of many faces. Graham Greene's *Brighton Rock* gives a wonderful picture of the town in the 1930s, with its background of promise of pleasures possible only at the seaside, whether cheap and cheerful or expensive and exclusive. There were also underlying hints of sexual improprieties, and the violence of the racecourse gangs up on the Downs, which sometimes spilled over into the town, like the clashes between mods and rockers 20 years later, all giving it an edge whilst ordinary, everyday lives continued regardless.

Perhaps the least-known aspect of Brighton encountered by the day-tripper was its industrial one. Railway-locomotive and motor-coach-body construction (in Hove) were just two examples of heavy engineering carried on locally. In this respect Brighton had much in common with the industrial towns and cities of the north. Like them it had its Corporation trams and like many of them it gave serious consideration to removing them in the 1930s. The decision to do so was duly taken, and the first trolleybuses took up work in May 1939. However, matters were not that clear-cut, for since 1915 Thomas Tilling had been operating motor buses in the town, to say nothing of Southdown, which had a monopoly of long-distance services to other parts of Sussex. On my visits to Brighton, usually in a Southdown coach — a Hove-built Harrington-bodied Leyland Tiger TS7 or TS8 — in the days immediately after World War 2, my perception was that the town services were operated by red and cream motor and trolleybuses, and it was only later that I realised that these belonged to two quite separate concerns.
The elders of the Corporation had long hankered after running their own bus services (electric trams had been

**One of Brighton Corporation's 1939 AEC Regents, considered by the author an 'elegant example of the bus-builder's art'. The Vauxhall Velox (or Wyvern) dates this view to the early 1950s.**

inaugurated in 1901), but the nearest they got for some years was receiving payments from Thomas Tilling, the money largely being used on the upkeep of the roads over which the buses ran.

Trolleybuses came early to Brighton, experiments using the tram overhead being conducted in 1913/14, but nothing came of them, at least not for another 25 years. Eventually, in 1939 a tripartite agreement was reached between Southdown, Brighton Hove & District (created in 1935 as a direct subsidiary of Thomas Tilling Ltd) and the Corporation, the last replacing its trams with a fleet of 44 trolleybuses and 21 motor buses, which took up work almost simultaneously with the outbreak of war.

My inability to distinguish between the vehicles of Brighton Hove & District (BH&D) and those of the Corporation has some excuse, for there was, indeed, very little difference. Not only were the liveries identical but all bore the same fleetname, those of the Corporation carrying the in addition the borough crest. However, the vehicle-purchasing policies varied greatly. Thomas Tilling had been particularly keen to expand in Brighton, for, having entered into an agreement with the London General Omnibus Co to keep within a defined area there (an irksome restriction) the company wanted other outlets. As it happened this was my area, the three Tilling garages being Catford, Bromley and Croydon. In the 1930s identical buses worked in Croydon and Brighton, but I was not impressed, for not only were they elderly; they looked and sounded it. These were AEC Regents, with petrol engines and Tilling-designed and -built bodies. The shorter version, the ST, had an open staircase, and whilst the longer STL was totally enclosed and of more rounded appearance, it still looked old-fashioned. In truth by the time I got to know Brighton the similarity was less marked, for the STs in London had been withdrawn and the STLs modernised and in some cases rebodied.

Brighton Corporation also went in for AECs, but these were utterly different. In the 10 years since the emergence of the Tilling ST, double-deck bus bodies had become vastly more elegant and streamlined. Brighton Corporation chose Weymann to supply both the motor-bus and trolleybus bodies. In their well-proportioned red and cream livery, with generous destination indicators and, in the case of the motor buses, with that almost timeless AEC radiator, they were true classics. Indeed, whenever I come across the preserved example, FUF 63, which has been a regular on the rally circuit for very many years, I find myself wondering if there has ever been a more elegant example of the bus-builder's art. The 1939 Regents not only looked good; they *were* good, serving the town for over 20 years. The Corporation got its money's worth out of the trolleybuses too, for they lasted until 1961. Eight similar vehicles, delivered to BH&D in 1939, were stored for the duration of the war, finally taking up work in 1944-6; along with a trio of similar BUTs received in 1948 these were the Tilling Group's only trolleybuses.

After the war things changed considerably, BH&D having become a typical Tilling concern, standardising on ECW-bodied Bristols and being nationalised with the rest of that organisation in 1948. Then in 1970 the Corporation adopted a predominantly light-blue livery with a good deal of white. Following the merger of the BET and state-owned THC interests and the creation of the National Bus Company the adoption of the rather dull NBC leaf green for Southdown — which absorbed BH&D — ensured that red buses would no longer be seen on the streets of Brighton. This would not perhaps have caused so much regret had both the Corporation's blue and NBC's green worn well. But they didn't, and the pride which had been there in the 1940s and '50s seemed to vanish too.

Today the picture has changed utterly. In 1986, in anticipation of NBC privatisation, Southdown was divided, resulting in the formation the Brighton & Hove Bus and Coach Company (in actual fact the old BH&D company reactivated), and a return to red and cream. Go-Ahead acquired the company from its original management buy-out team in 1993. Then four years later Go-Ahead also bought Brighton Transport, the direct descendant of the Corporation tram, trolley and motor-bus operation. In the 21st century Brighton, Hove and the surrounding areas are served by a company which is in the forefront of innovation, with imaginative liveries and advertising, a fare structure which sees more and more people attracted from their cars, and a route network which extends way beyond the city deep into the Sussex countryside and surrounding towns.

An endearing feature of modern Brighton buses is their names. So many famous people have lived in Brighton over the years that it has proved possible to bestow names on practically the entire fleet without exhausting the list. Thus one might find *Prince Regent* swinging around the Steine pursued by *Adam Faith*, passing *Lord Olivier* and *Dame Anna Neagle* heading in the opposite direction. The company may not be owned by the Corporation any more, but it is certainly one of which Brightonians can be proud.

**In the late 1950s and early 1960s Brighton favoured Leyland Titan PD2s with Weymann bodywork. Twenty were delivered in 1959. They were 61-seaters.**

***Right:*** **Brighton & Hove's first low-floor double-deckers were Dennis Tridents. This East Lancs-bodied bus, from an initial batch of 20 delivered in 1999, is named after Magnus Volk, creator of Brighton's seafront electric railway, which opened in 1883.**

***Below:*** **More recently Brighton & Hove has standardised on Scanias such as this 2003 OmniDekka, with bodywork by East Lancs. Sir Edward Burne-Jones was a Victorian artist.**

*Left:* **Brighton & Hove's coastal route to Eastbourne offers spectacular views. A 2006 OmniDekka illustrates the point as it climbs out of Eastbourne in April 2009. The bus is named after James Gray, a local historian who died in 1998.**

One of the most attractive bus rides to be experienced anywhere in the UK is on Brighton & Hove's 12/12A route running east along the cliff tops out of Brighton, down to Rottingdean, up again through Peacehaven, then down again to the ancient port of Newhaven. Next it passes through Seaford and then enters what was designated in 2009 as a National Park, culminating in breathtaking views from the top of Beachy Head, before a precipitous descent into Eastbourne.

If Brighton is the most cosmopolitan of the UK's seaside towns and cities, Eastbourne has a reputation of being one of the most sedate. I'm not sure this is justified any more, but it is an altogether different sort of place, although the two do have quite a lot in common. Each has a pier. Brighton used to have two, but the West Pier, long neglected and, to tell the truth, although elegant, rather boring, has suffered a series of disasters and is now reduced to an iron skeleton. On the other hand the Palace Pier, which no-one could ever call elegant, goes from strength to strength — noisy, vibrant, garish and all that a pier should be. Eastbourne's pier is nothing short of beautiful, matching the best of the town's seafront architecture.

Eastbourne was unique amongst South Coast resort municipal bus operators in that it never operated trams. Instead in 1902 the Corporation persuaded Parliament to grant it powers to run motor buses on its streets; this was a really rather remarkable state of affairs, for the town was not renowned for indulging in revolutionary activities and chancing its arm on untried technologies. So on 12 April 1903 began the very first municipal motor-bus service, not just in the UK but in the world. It ran from the railway station to The Meads, beneath the Downs at the western end of the promenade.

There being no precedent in the local-authority world as to which department should be put in charge, Mr J. K. Brydes, Borough Electrical Engineer, was given the responsibility, overseen by the Electric Light Committee. Private horse-bus services had been operating for some years, and there were those in the town who hankered after a tram system. Indeed, the council received a deputation of citizens to this effect later in 1903, but the appointment in 1906 as Transport Manager of Percy Ellison, formerly with Leeds Corporation, ensured not only that the Corporation motor-bus services established a monopoly but that they

***Above:*** **Many of Eastbourne's buses enjoyed long lives, among them this 1931 Leyland Titan TD1, seen in service in 1949, its last year of operation. It had Leyland's own classic six-bay body.**

***Right:*** **Two preserved buses recalling the past glory of Eastbourne Corporation. The double-decker was one of eight AEC Regent IIIs with constant-mesh gearboxes and Bruce-built East Lancs bodies. Behind is the solitary Regal III delivered in 1950; it was bodied by East Lancs.**

expanded. By the time Mr Ellison retired, in 1939, we were virtually in the modern era, and some of the buses he introduced survived into the 1960s.

Trams did eventually come to Eastbourne, in 1954, when a narrow-gauge line opened to the east of the town centre between Prince's Park and The Crumbles. I remember it well and, like many enthusiasts, hoped that the council would allow it to expand. It wouldn't, so in 1969 the tramway upped sticks – or rather tracks, overhead and trams – and took itself some 175 miles to the west, setting up at Seaton, in Devon, where it has prospered mightily. Eastbourne's loss was East Devon's gain.

The Eastbourne fleet when I first got to know it well in the 1960s, living just outside the town in Hailsham but working in it at a seafront hotel, consisted entirely of Leylands and AECs. Eight Crossleys were bought in 1948, but they went relatively early, being withdrawn in 1962/3. One tends to think of Crossleys as being very much confined to the North of England, but they were not unknown in the South, two other municipals, Maidstone and Portsmouth, buying the make. Double-deckers enjoyed a vitual monopoly in Eastbourne, but the exceptions were particularly interesting. The newer of the two was a rather elegant AEC Regal of 1950 with an East Lancs body, whilst the other was one of the oldest buses in ordinary service anywhere in the country, being an all-Leyland Lion dating from 1939. Its survival was all the more notable in that its four companions, delivered at the same time, were almost immediately requisitioned for military service and never seen again in Eastbourne.
I used to come across it pottering around the town, a typical elderly resident, not overdoing it, being used for

***Left:* Eastbourne Corporation's last open-toppers were five Leyland Titan PD1s with East Lancs bodies. New in 1946 as the fleet's first diesel-engined buses, they were de-roofed in 1961/2 and operated until 1968.**

private hire and rush-hour reliefs, a remarkable survivor. When it was finally withdrawn, in 1967, it passed into preservation. The Regal was equally long-lived, not being withdrawn until 1978, but even then its Eastbourne career was not over, for it was bought back in 1993.

There was little resemblance between the Brighton and Eastbourne fleets, East Lancs providing the bodywork for practically all the Eastbourne half-cabs and, indeed, the Roadliners, Panthers and Atlanteans which succeeded them. East Lancs bodies were seen in Brighton, but until the 1970s only in Southdown colours. However, there were six notable exceptions to the East Lancs rule in Eastbourne, these being AEC Regents delivered in 1946/7. These had Weymann bodies, the first, a Mk II Regent, being just about identical to the 1939 Brighton deliveries. Later Regents were Mk IIIs, and the bodywork, like that on the postwar Brighton examples, differed in a number of ways, the most notable being that they were of four-bay layout; I never thought them quite as handsome as the earlier buses.

From 1946 until 1963 Eastbourne bought nothing but Regents, eight more Mk IIIs in 1951, then 22 Mk Vs in the years 1961-3. Thereafter the Leyland Titan found favour, 15 PD2A/30s delivered in 1966/7 being Eastbourne's final half-cabs. It was not unusual for an Eastbourne half-cab to last around 20 years, particularly the early postwar examples, and they always looked immaculate. Eastbourne's livery was blue and primrose, but later many of the half-cabs were repainted in a predominantly cream

***Below:* In the 1970s open-top services in Eastbourne were provided by Southdown. Here, in the summer of 1976, a 1963 Lodekka FS6B convertible, inherited from Brighton Hove & District, unloads alongside a 1967 East Lancs-bodied PD2 in the Corporation fleet.**

livery with a blue stripe beneath the lower-deck windows, an 'EBC' logo replacing the traditional 'EASTBOURNE CORPORATION' flanking the town's coat of arms.

Not surprisingly for a coastal resort, Eastbourne possessed a fleet (albeit small) of open-toppers, five 1938 Regents being so converted in the 1950s and serving until 1961/2, when they were replaced by five 1946 Leyland PD1s. These were all withdrawn before the 1968 season began, and the fleet then found itself bereft of such vehicles. This was an odd situation for a seaside fleet, particularly as Southdown had just put into service a number of convertible Leyland PD3s which were working the service along the seafront and then climbing high to the top of Beachy Head.

The end of the 1960s marked the end of the heyday of municipal bus operation in Eastbourne. Increasing car use was cutting into receipts. The first one-man buses, three Daimler Roadliners, arrived in 1967/8 and were found to be pretty useless, and the Leyland Panthers that followed were not much better. In 1972 came the first Atlanteans, which turned out to be the forerunners of a large fleet of the type, which in the early 1980s was bolstered by second-hand acquisitions from Ipswich and Southampton. The long-established Churchdale Road garage became outdated and unsuitable for dealing with rear-engined buses, and closed in 1980, being replaced by new premises in Birch Road. Corporation vehicles never enjoyed the luxury of a bus station (unlike those of Southdown, which at one time had the use not only of a bus station but also a beautiful art-deco coach station, both now wantonly demolished), but the railway station was a convenient gathering-point.

Deregulation in 1986 meant that at last Corporation buses could reach the top of Beachy Head, and they also ventured out of the town, to my former home at Hailsham and well beyond to many Sussex destinations which had once been the preserve of Southdown. Livery variations, with dark blue predominating, appeared and disappeared.

By the mid-2000s Eastbourne Buses was among the declining number of municipally owned bus operators in the UK. However, it was far from healthy. Sale was inevitable, and the employees and most other observers hoped that it would pass into the hands of Go-Ahead, owner of Brighton & Hove. But Go-Ahead was not prepared to offer more than £2.85 million, whilst Stagecoach came up with £3.7 million. Even this was considered low, one MP commenting that Eastbourne Buses had been 'given away for nothing'. However, MPs are not always very realistic when it comes to handing over hard cash as opposed to wishful thinking, and at the end of 2008 Stagecoach duly took over — a sad end for the world's first and longest-lived municipally owned bus operation, and also the end of municipal bus ownership in South East England.

**New to Eastbourne in 1994 was this DAF DB250 with 77-seat Northern Counties Palatine II body. It is seen in 2009, a few months after the business had been purchased by Stagecoach.**

*Above:* **Among the more modern buses in the Eastbourne fleet in its final days were 10 MAN 14.220s with 40-seat MCV Evolution bodies, delivered in the summer of 2006. Behind in this view near the railway station is a 1998 Dennis Dart SLF with Plaxton Pointer body.**

*Right:* **When it took over in Eastbourne Stagecoach promised to invest in new buses. The first were 12 Alexander Dennis Enviro300 44-seaters.**

# Scottish Titans

No Scottish operators bought new examples of Leyland's integral Titan, but in the 1990s and 2000s a number of former London examples found new homes north of the border, as **Billy Nicol** illustrates.

***Right:*** **Stagecoach was the biggest Scottish Titan user, and its first examples were allocated to the A1 Service fleet in Ayrshire in early 1995 to replace older buses acquired with the A1 business. Many entered service in London red, as apparent from this view at Irvine Cross.**

***Below:*** **Stagecoach Western used Titans to compete with First in Glasgow in 1997. Here one loads in the city centre for the southern suburb of Newton Mearns. Most Titans, including this one, had Gardner engines.**

*Left:* **The centre exit door was not used by Stagecoach in Scotland, and some Titans were rebuilt as single-door buses. This is a Fife Scottish bus, seen in Dunfermline in 1997. The Fife company had in fact ordered three Titans in 1978, but the order was cancelled because of Leyland's inability to deliver on time.**

*Below left:* **Clydeside, when part of British Bus, received a small number of London Titans (and Metrobuses), primarily for school services. The company had a bright livery, as seen on this 17-year-old bus returning to the depot in Johnstone from a school run in 1996.**

*Below:* **Guide Friday operated Titans on a service between Edinburgh city centre and the airport, in competition with the established Lothian Buses route. Prominent route branding left passengers in no doubt as to what the Titans were doing.**

*Above:* **On more typical Guide Friday work is this open-top Titan, owned by Stagecoach Bluebird, operating a city tour of Perth. The photograph was taken in 2000.**

*Below:* **Perthshire operator Earnside of Glenfarg uses a yellow livery, which seems appropriate on a Titan employed on school services. A 1981 bus leaves the company's depot in 2002.**

***Left:*** **Rennies of Dunfermline bought Titans for school and contract operations. Among its purchases was this former Stagecoach London bus, seen at the company's depot in 2003. The Rennies business was acquired by Stagecoach in 2008.**

***Left:*** **With interest growing in the concept of yellow school buses, Stagecoach repainted a number of Titans yellow, with appropriate lettering that cleverly incorporated the company's logo. This is a Stagecoach Western bus, seen in Glasgow in 2005.**

***Below:*** **Titans lasted long enough to receive the current version of Stagecoach's corporate livery, as demonstrated by this 20-year-old bus seen on a local service in Ayr in the summer of 2004.**

# Further round the bend

**In which Robert E. Jowitt, on extended pursuits of articulated buses, finds himself on, perhaps, the brink of insanity.**

*All photographs by the author.*

"The mad man! He's here!" Thus violently, by the terror in Sweetheart's voice, was I awoken at an unearthly hour of the morning from uneasy slumber, head on arms over a table in the restaurant at Aachen Hauptbahnhof. "The lunatic! Now!"

Indeed he was. Sitting at our table, inches away from us, fixing us with that awful deadly unwinking stare. We had seen him earlier, at other tables, fixing other passengers with that same dreadful gaze. I guess Sweetheart, like myself, had fallen asleep, over the table, and been woken up by his horrid arrival.

It is my habit, expected of me, I believe, by my readers, to start my essays in these pages with some dramatic paragraphs, and I hope — from adventures in the frozen February of 1963 — the above will serve.

Sweetheart and I had come up from Ostend to Aachen on a night train. I must suppose that I knew, with knowledge now forgotten, that the Aachen Hauptbahnhof restaurant was open all night, and that we could not catch a train onwards thence to our destination until the early hours of the morrow. The waiter, presumably used to the scenario, told us the lunatic was harmless, but contrived somehow to move him on.

I had been in Aachen before, for trams, but had delighted especially in the first unique taste of the Fatherland, the wares shouted by a splendid man who trod the platforms of the Hauptbahnhof with a steaming trolley of *heiße Wurst*, or hot sausage. I would not mention such matters of 45 or more years ago, save only that Aachen has recently come to my attention again — with what might be further insanity?

Just as I like to start my *Buses Yearbook* essay with a bold piece of narrative, so also I sometimes enjoy returning to follow some subject I have visited hitherto; which here must include proposals — then unachieved — in 'Off the Wall' (*Buses Yearbook 2010*) as a continuation of 'Round the Bend' in *Buses Yearbook 2004*. As both books are readily obtainable at any decent bus rally I will not here tell again of my origins of affection for articulated buses except for noting that I had encountered a three-part, or (as my Luxembourg psychiatrist friend, known in these pages as SP, described it) 'tripartite'.

Now, having lately heard of half a dozen tripartites delivered to Aachen I prevailed upon SP to accompany me, primarily for my pleasure in her company and for her to prevent me from stepping off pavements into traffic coming from the unfamiliar left, so that we could together enjoy the

**A Van Hool AGG300 tripartite in Aachen. The AGG300 is 24.8m long.**

**Similar Van Hools are in operation in Luxembourg, this one with Sales-Lentz.**

wonderful railway from Luxembourg to Liège and onward up the Vesdre valley, old international main-line delight of my teenage years, through to Aachen. There I would reward her with six tripartites and, of course, *heiße Wurst…*

SP was not averse to tripartite enthusiasm and, before we could set out on the proposed jaunt, had sent me from Luxembourg an SMS message as follows: "I've just boarded a tripartite bus with 'essai scientifique' written on the front! How thrilling! I wonder if the passengers are part of the experiment." Just the sort of message to reassure me that SP was exactly the sort of girl to take bus-hunting — then, a few minutes later: "It was a hybrid bus — electric with generator in the back. Made in Switzerland and Germany, and the engine in America."

Before SP and I set out for Aachen, she, not trusting my age-old well-tried theory that there will always be a pot-house with rooms somewhere near the station, elected to scour the internet for an Aachen hotel. And found one, alleged to be near the bus station, and booked rooms accordingly. Then, booking confirmed, she realised she had booked the wrong night, this night, when we were still in Luxembourg, so internetted again to say we were actually arriving the next night. And checked this out, the following morning, by mobile phone from the train while I admired the Luxembourg scenery, that all was well.

What was not so well was that from Liège the glorious Vesdre Valley railway of my formative years was no longer a through route to Aachen, being bypassed by a mostly in-tunnel Euro-style affair; but we travelled by the still-bewitching old line as far as we could, ending, on a branch off it, at Eupen. This was by no means objectionable, as I had often read of Eupen and its trams which, by wars and treaties, had been variously Belgian or German (I mean the trams themselves had actually had their nationality changed) — not that there were any there now.
SP (a professional translator) was pleased enough with the town, as it is the district of the third recognised Belgian tongue — not French, not Flemish, but German, so she could experience the reality with café staff. And it boasts a splendid Baroque church. And thence we pressed on, in a fine articulated bus, towards Aachen, over handsome uplands but sufficiently thinly populated even today to make one wonder why ever anyone built a tram line across them, past an altered but plainly recognisable tram depot and a border post with vast queuing areas for cars and lorries abandoned now by the EU regime.

From the Aachen bus station we found our hotel and, passing the dining room on the way to the reception, saw what from the rear looked like a very old man more or less fixed against one of the tables — and then encountered the landlady. She, bulbous-eyed and with leonine mane of white hair, once having discovered our identity, launched into a furious attack on SP, three or four times repeated, for having kept her awake awaiting us until three o'clock in the morning, occasionally turning to me as if for confirmation even though SP said (with strict disregard for truth) that I couldn't speak German, until finally, realising that we would walk out, save only that, in English, SP said to me that the maniac already had her card-number, the maniac became amiable and gave us our keys.

***Above:*** **Luxembourg operator Weber runs this bus with a separate passenger trailer — a combination which took the author by surprise.**

***Right:*** **Tripartite trolleybus — with a tram in the background — in Zurich. Five of these Hess-built Lightram 3 models were delivered in 2007/8. They are 25m long and can carry up to 200 people.**

When we had found our rooms and recovered a little we set out to explore, passing the very old man still stuck moribund against the dining-room table. The streets abounded with delightful statues and a constant splendid flow of buses — but if there were plenty of normal articulateds there was never a tripartite. Next morning, after a good breakfast (with the old man fortunately removed from the dining room) I borrowed the old woman's phone book. Thank goodness she herself was absent, and an amiable if harassed minion charged us for only one night, and SP rang the depot. Ha, the tripartites didn't operate during school holidays — but, after some appeal by SP, if we went to the depot, a tripartite would be exhibited to us! A kindly bus driver told us which stop we58needed, and off we set. In truth, a tripartite was out, waiting for us, and we were driven several circuits and voluptuous bends round the depot perimeter with great panache and allowed to take any photos we wished. What excellent hospitality! And the ordinary bus we caught back to the city was in the hands of the driver who had told us where to catch the outward bus, and he well pleased to see we had successfully followed his directions.

Time for us to take a train back to Luxembourg, noting that the celebrated restaurant had been converted to booking and enquiry offices and replaced by 'fast-food-outlets' and

**The four-axle artics in St Gallen are MAN Lion's City GXL models, 20.45m in length. St Gallen was the first customer for the GXL.**

that there was no longer a vendor of hot sausages on the platform, so I could not fulfil my promise! Tragedy.

In Luxembourg I soon discovered that what had been the one and only tripartite on my previous visit plus the new 'essai scientifique' was not all. Another, hitherto unknown to me, caterpillared past, and hardly had it gone but it came back the other way — which no, it couldn't, so there must be two of it! There were now, in fact, with various operators, at least, I estimated, half a dozen. I managed also to capture that vast three-axle double-deck which, glimpsed previously, had hitherto eluded me close up, plus a further new delight, a common bus hauling a passenger trailer, a practice I had believed long since EU-outlawed. Meanwhile, further convinced, as I had long felt, that the best way to catch photographically the complex movements of any artics in Luxembourg was from a great height, I attacked the municipal library at the Hamilius bus station in the centre of Luxembourg.

Émile Hamilius (1897-1971) was, so SP told me, Mayor of Luxembourg City 1946-63 and played football for Luxembourg at the 1920 Antwerp Olympics, but I rather fear his name is mostly now synonymous with 'bus station'. The Hamilius library receptionist despatched me on a long hot trek to municipal offices near the station, where the next receptionist spoke on the phone to the authority to whom I was bidden to seek permission, who then on the phone spoke to me and bade me return to Hamilius where all would be well — via another long hot trek — and all was in truth well. The porter conveyed me up to the ninth or so floor, decided I was *bona fide* and not going to attempt suicide, and left me to it. I spent as enjoyable an hour as ever I have spent, even though the tripartites stayed in a straight line outside instead of wriggling into the bus station.

From Luxembourg I took the train to Zürich, and, in a frightful cloudburst (apparently huge hailstones were smashing car windscreens in other parts of Switzerland) saw the trams, some of which I must have seen 40 years ago when new, and the tripartite trolleybuses which were the target of my visit. I found, by walking from the station, a clean, boring (chain) hotel, and in the morning a viewpoint, known to me from before, for the trolleybuses.

I later took a train to St Gallen, for the other great target of my visit. Which was the MAN Lion's City articulated on *four* axles. In my youth, in encounters in Germany, and though ever devoted to trams rather than buses, I had been fascinated by this arrangement, but believed it long abandoned. But if it had made a comeback I had to see it!

Thank Heaven I can speak enough German to understand Schweizerdeutsch, and some chaps obviously bus-uniformed round an outdoor café table, upon my enquiry, produced a *Bildfahrplan* and told me to the

***Above:*** **Stuttgart operates four-axle artics – Mercedes-Benz Citaro CapaCitys. The CapaCity is 19.5m long, compared with 17.9m for a standard three-axle Citaro artic.**

***Right:*** **Round the bend, full lock, in St Gallen.**

minute where and when it would arrive. Thus I travelled on a spectacularly long vehicle through trim Swiss suburbia and a view over the blue, yacht-speckled Bodensee, and was told I was lucky to ride on it, as it was as often in the workshop as out on the road. Note that one of the reasons I had not written of this a year previously for *Buses Yearbook* was that it had not then, so I gathered, been delivered. It is perhaps relevant to add that St Gallen boasts or hosts a fine flock of normal articulated trolleybuses and, to add to the fun, several three-axle double-deck Post Buses of Luxembourg mammoth bulk.

I proceeded then to Luzern, where, in another spectacular cloudburst, I saw trolleybuses hauling trailers (having been told by a friend that I *must* see these!) and, what I hadn't been told, there were tripartite trolleybuses too. Luzern, cloudburst or not, was ever too touristy a place to please me. I returned to Zürich and on to Basel and via Luxembourg to home. Well pleased, it might be supposed. In due time, however, other matters came to light.

First I heard of the delivery of more four-axle artics, in this case to Stuttgart, Germany.

Second, from a timetable I had picked up in St Gallen, I noted the existence of what they choose to describe as a 'Lightram' — a term borrowed from tripartite trolleybuses built by Hess — but in this case, so far as I could gather from a telephone call in Schweizerdeutsch, a 'home-made' interpretation of the ilk — but why hadn't I spotted it while I was there?

Thirdly, while foot-slogging — or tramming — in Zürich I had spotted a hotel which would far better have suited my photographic intentions than that dull dump where I had ended in the cloudburst.

And fourth, still in Zürich, I had missed visiting the Bucheggplatz, the most complex trolleybus overhead layout in Europe if not the whole world.

Fifth, the shutter on my new second-hand Minolta proved afterwards to have been playing me false. Providence be praised, Aachen and Hamilius emerged more or less intact, but much of the rest was lost.

Items one to four I might have decided to defer to next year or sometime, never, but number five was not to be tolerated …

Two months later I started on Stuttgart. The four-axles were said to be working out of Möhringen and Vaihingen. When I was last in these places, 45 or so years previously, the inter-urban tram services had some of the oldest cars in Germany, while the rest of Stuttgart had some of the newest, and the cleanest. None of this now applied, and nor, upon enquiry of a Möhringen driver, did four-axles, but I was advised to try Vaihingen, which indeed produced several.

Already depressed, however, by the light industry and suburbia which now abounded in this district, I contented myself with photographs rather than exploring the route the four-axles served, and retired down to Stuttgart to travel the 42 where I had spotted one working. On the map the route looked good and proved in truth to sample almost primitive villages in its ups and downs along with

**The varying floor levels of St Gallen's 'home-made' three-section trolleybus give a clue to the vehicle's origin as a conventional articulated trolley, to which a rear section has been added. The NAW/Hess vehicle was new in 1991 and rebuilt in 2006.**

***Above:*** **Room with a view. St Gallen by night, with a conventional articulated trolleybus, a Polish-built Solaris Trollino 18.**

***Right:*** **St Gallen, with a choice collection featuring a Swiss PostBus three-axle double-decker (top), two PostBus artics and, nearest the camera, a St Gallen artic. Passing by is a four-axle Lion's City.**

heavy Kaiser Wilhelm architecture, well worth the ride, even with only one four-axle on the timetable.

I decided to return to the other, at St Gallen (where, while I was waiting for it, the Lightram was the first vehicle to pass me) and to explore the other end of its route which, with that dire attention to detail which only the Swiss can do so well, was even worse suburbia and industrial estates than I might have caught around Vaihingen, save at the last it emerged into ancient rural Swiss, even to cows with bells ringing round their necks. The Lightram, onto which luck favoured me an instant connection when I abandoned the four-axle, proved, save for passage of a sensational gorge, little better. The Lightram, in my view, has its rear section, suitably low-floor as may now be deemed desirable, at an uncouth-looking level with the rest of the trolleybus, arguably outside and certainly within.

I spent the rest of the day — and the night — in a very expensive hotel with a bottle of wine, a packet of tobacco (smoking is permitted still in some Swiss hotels) two cameras and three lenses, and a top-floor view of the bus station outside the *Hauptbahnhof* … and have seldom enjoyed my pursuit better!

Then I pressed on to Luzern, which, in brilliant sunshine, was as touristic and undesirable as it had been in cloudburst, and so back to Zürich, to the hotel I had spotted last time, and had already ordered a convenient room for two nights, suitably equipping it with wine, tobacco, and cameras. In intervals from this I took a tram through heavy bourgeois Swiss architecture to the Bucheggplatz trolleybus junction. This is a huge tree-clad roundabout with tram and trolleybus stops in the centre, the motor traffic around it so deadly you must approach by pedestrian bridges almost designed to afford perfect view of the overhead complex — and for free, unlike those hotels!

After other Zürich tram adventures I carried on to Schaffhausen for a brief glimpse of its one trolleybus line, on which I didn't trouble to ride as its route closely followed the bleak section of railway I had just experienced — not even for the sake of the Rheinfall, which looked smaller than I remembered it in 1963, anyway. The trolleybuses, true, were pretty enough, but I remembered the archaic trams.

So on again, for a re-take in Basel, and this time again in a high-price hotel, though as this was almost entirely tram-orientated I can't tell you anything about it here save only that I vastly enjoyed it and thought that my deceased aunt (at 90-plus), herself a serious traveller, would appreciate the way I was blowing her legacy! Which might well be counted an insanity.

I felt no need to re-visit Aachen, I had no wish to see again the mad lady of the hotel, or to discover if the moribund old man in the dining room was sitting staring with unblinking 1963 eyes.

And as for the hot sausage and my promise to SP …

Well, we were travelling up country in Luxembourg in her car – in search of quite other game, or in fact the 1820-ish works of the never-completed Meuse–Moselle Canal — when I called a halt at a roadside snack bar, the kitchen a caravan and the dining room a derelict and possibly third- or fourth-hand and probably ex-German-city but nevertheless tidy articulated bus. And the establishment was offering hot sausage. I do not like to make a promise, however far round the bend, to so charming a lady as SP, and prove unable to fulfil it; here the problem was solved, the promise fulfilled. Even though the dead bus was not tripartite …

And there were no lunatics present, unless, of course, you count the presence of Robert E. Jowitt …

***Left:*** **Four sets of wires, all initially heading in the same direction, over Bucheggplatz in Zürich. The Mercedes/ABB O405 trolleybus is from a batch of 43 delivered in 1994/5.**

***Below:*** **A snack bar up-country, north of Luxembourg City. Jowitt has not pursued its ancestry but can confirm that it serves excellent hot sausages.**

# Devon and Cornwall in the 1980s

The 1980s was a period of change in the bus industry. **Mark Bailey** illustrates some of the variety to be found three decades ago in England's far South West.

*Right:* **Plymouth is the biggest city in the South West, and in the 1980s most local services were provided by Plymouth City Transport. PCT bought Leyland Atlanteans for over 20 years and the final 36, delivered between 1979 and 1981, had East Lancs bodywork. One of these is pictured in wintry conditions in March 1987 climbing away from Lower Compton. Plymouth was from 1970 the only municipal bus operation in Devon. The operation was purchased by Go-Ahead in 2009.**

*Right:* **From 1982 some Plymouth-based buses in the Western National fleet sported a variation of National Bus Company livery incorporating the Citybus logo used by Plymouth City Transport. Leaving Bretonside bus station for Tavistock in October 1986 is an ECW-Bodied Bristol VRT. Co-operation between Plymouth City Transport and Western National would soon turn to competition.**

*Left:* **In the early 1980s Western National acquired a batch of Daimler Fleetlines from London Transport. This Metro-Cammell-bodied example, converted, like the rest, to single-door, is seen in Camborne bus station in August 1981. The Cornish Fairways branding was Western National's attempt at giving its vehicles in the county a local identity. Note the advertisement for TDK tape cassettes, a sound-recording medium now consigned to history.**

*Right:* **Devon General re-emerged on 1 January 1983 when the Western National Omnibus Co was split into four new companies — the others being North Devon, Southern National and a slimmed-down Western National. The new Devon General covered virtually the same area as its predecessor had before being absorbed by Western National in 1971. In the mid-1980s Devon General pioneered the large-scale operation of minibuses, replacing most of its fleet of full-size service buses. Pictured on layover in Exeter's Paris Street bus station in July 1986 are two Ford Transits converted from vans — that on the left by Midland Red's Carlyle Works and that on the right by Robin Hood.**

*Left:* **In stark contrast to the minibuses which dominated later in the decade, the Devon General fleet of the early 1980s included this Willowbrook-bodied Atlantean, one of six new in 1966, when the company was part of the British Electric Traction group. This style of body was relatively unusual, particularly so in NBC fleets. The photograph was taken in 1983, by which time the bus was showing its age.**

*Left:* **A well-loaded Devon General Leyland Leopard heads for Exeter on the South Devon Express in the summer of 1984. The style of Willowbrook body, the 003, was developed specifically for the National Bus Company, this coach being one of nine 49-seaters delivered to Western National in 1980.**

*Right:* **In the new North Devon fleet buses were branded as 'Red Bus', although the fleetname looked odd when applied to the old NBC leaf-green livery on buses which had not been repainted. A rather battered Roe-bodied Leyland Atlantean of 1961 makes the point in Barnstaple in February 1984.**

*Left:* **In the early 1980s Brixham Coaches, trading as Burton's, sported a livery of dark green and white, as worn by this smart 21-year-old Duple (Midland)-bodied Bedford SB3, seen on a local service to the Sharkham Point holiday camp in June 1982. Burton's would later be purchased by Transit Holdings, owner of Devon General.**

*Left:* **This little gem was 35 years old and still in regular service when photographed in September 1985 in St Columb Major, Cornwall. An Austin K8VC with 12-seat Tiverton coachwork, it was new in 1950 and acquired by Chapman of Rosenannon in 1966. It is seen outside the parish church waiting to depart on the Wednesdays-only market-day service back to its home village.**

*Below:* **Flora Motors of Helston operated a service to the village of Manaccan. Seen in February 1985 is an ECW-bodied Bristol LH6L which came from Greater Manchester Transport. New in 1974, it was one of six in the GMT fleet and had been ordered by Wigan Corporation. The flat-glass windscreens were unusual on an ECW-bodied LH of this period, NBC having specified curved screens since 1970. Flora was acquired by Truronian at the end of 1987.**

*Above:* **For many years Grenville Motors was the largest independent operator in Cornwall, running services in the Camborne, Redruth and Falmouth areas and also reaching Helston and Penzance. Seen in Camborne in February 1982, heading for its home village of Troon, is a Willowbrook-bodied Bedford YRQ which had been new to Barton Transport in 1971. The Grenville business was purchased by Western National in 1988.**

*Below:* **Harvey's was based in Mousehole, Cornwall, and ran the service to Newlyn and Penzance in conjunction with Western National. In the 1980s the service was maintained by a pair of Bristol LHS6Ls, the short length being required to navigate the tight corners of this picturesque fishing village. Seen in Penzance in August 1981 is the older of the two, new in 1977, which had Marshall bodywork.**

*Right:* **Kinsmans of Bodmin operated a service which linked the north Cornwall villages of Polzeath and Rock with Wadebridge. In August 1983 the regular vehicle was a 1972 ECW-bodied Bristol RELL6L acquired from Alder Valley. It is pictured at the Wadebridge end of the route.**

*Left:* **Launceston Car Hire provided the local service in this hilly Cornish town. Seen passing the remains of Launceston Castle in July 1983 is a Park Royal-bodied AEC Swift which had been new to London Country in 1970.**

*Below:* **North Cornwall Cars of Langdon Cross operated three Leyland Panthers that had been new to Lincoln City Transport in 1970. One is pictured in July 1983, arriving in Launceston on the Tuesdays-only market-day service from North Petherwin. Roe built the 49-seat body.**

*Right:* **Based originally in the East Devon village of Whimple and later in Clyst Honiton, Red Bus Services was the trading name of Richard Holladay, who commenced operations in 1983 after purchasing and restoring this ex-Devon General Willowbrook-bodied Albion Nimbus. It is seen in August of that year in Exeter after arriving on the service from Feniton.**

*Below right:* **In 1909 the Kingsbridge–Salcombe route saw the first bus service to be operated by the Great Western Railway. Pictured sporting chocolate and cream GWR livery in September 1986 is a Tally Ho! ECW-bodied Bristol RELL6G acquired from Devon General. It is passing through the South Hams village of Loddiswell on service 603 to Kingsbridge, from where it will continue to Salcombe on service 606.**

*Below:* **The 'Rapide' services introduced at the start of the 1980s by Devon operator Trathen's were quickly embraced and expanded by National Express and became one of the success stories of the decade. Two of Trathen's fleet of striking Neoplan Skyliner double-deck coaches are pictured on layover in London in April 1984 before returning to Exeter and Plymouth. Trathen's went into receivership in September 1985, and the business, with a much-reduced fleet, was acquired by ATL, which owned Yelloway of Rochdale and UK Neoplan agent Carlton PSV Sales. Today Trathen's is owned by Parks of Hamilton.**

*Above:* **For a brief period in the mid-1980s a couple of Western National Leyland Olympians, upgraded with coach seating, wore National Express colours, representing possibly the most incongruous application of this livery (and providing a sharp contrast with the Neoplan Skyliners seen in the previous photograph). This 1983 ECW-bodied bus is pictured in December 1985 departing Plymouth's Bretonside bus station on the X1 to Penzance.**

*Below:* **The Isles of Scilly lie 30 miles off the Cornwall coast, and for many years Vic's Tours' vehicles were a familiar sight on St Mary's, the largest of the islands. As well as operating a 1949 Bedford OB, it had this 1951 Harrington-bodied Commer Avenger I still in regular service in the summer of 1984. It is seen parked in Hugh Town advertising an evening tour commencing at 7.50pm, lasting 1 hour and 10 minutes and costing £1.**

# Of Paramount importance

**David Jukes** tells the story of Plaxton's versatile 1980s market-leading coach, the Paramount.

*All photographs by the author.*

The Road Traffic Act 1980 removed regulation from coach services greater than 56km in length. It triggered a significant increase in the number of such services in the UK and represented one of the first steps in the Conservative Government's plans to deregulate the country's key industries.

Existing operators expanded their services to compete with a large number of newcomers, many of which had no previous associations with express coach travel. Companies soon realised that higher vehicle standards were required to stand out from their opposition. Continental coachbuilders initially provided the better-quality and distinctive-looking products called for, the then principal British-built ranges, Duple's Dominant and Plaxton's Supreme, appearing dated in comparison with contemporary European offerings.

Plaxton chose to address the UK coach market's needs with a new range named Paramount, which was launched at the 1982 Motor Show. It was styled by industrial-design specialist Ogle and initially offered in two heights — the conventional 3200 and high-floor 3500, the figures representing each variant's height in millimetres. Instead of the conventional aluminium panels used by Plaxton on its previous ranges the Paramount's steel frame was fitted with one-piece waist panels of Zintec-coated steel. Above these were rubber-gasket-mounted square-cornered windows of shallower depth than those fitted to the preceding Supreme range (save the shallow-glazed Supreme VI). Arguably the

The Paramount Concept —A New Generation of Luxury Coaches

Since 1927, Plaxtons have been building distinctive coaches for operators looking for the best their money could buy. Throughout this period, Plaxtons have earned a reputation for high quality coachwork linked to a personal customer service and are now proud to be known as the Great British Coachbuilders. Embracing the innovative technology of each new era, the company has remained at the forefront of the industry. Three gold medals and one silver medal recently awarded by the Institute of British Carriage and Automobile Manufacturers prove the success of our coachwork which can be seen all over the world. Following the highly successful Supreme Plaxtons now take another progressive step forward with a new generation in craftsmanship, style and luxury — the Paramount. Unique in design and comfort, the Paramount represents the company's continuing aim of providing the operator with the coach to meet his every need.

1927
Plaxtons first coach produced on Ford Model T chassis.

1948
Coach Body on Austin K4 chassis — Plaxtons popular post war design.

1964
Panorama bodied AEC Reliance — leading the way for the modern coaching industry.

1983
The new Paramount — Plaxtons once more setting the trend for the future.

2

3

**Plaxton reminded prospective buyers of the company's heritage in the original brochure for the Paramount.** courtesy R. E. GRAY

**A 1983 London Country Green Line Leyland Tiger unloads at Oxford's Gloucester Green bus station after arrival from London. It has a Mk I Paramount 3200 body, identifiable by the larger black dash panel, continuous slope of the waist trim between the windscreen and the narrow feature window in the second bay, and the lack of waist trim beneath the feature window. The coach is 11m long, the third bay being noticeably shorter than the remainder. The three-piece windscreen enabling the fitting of destination equipment and two-leaf passenger door identifies this as the Express version of the 3200.**

most eye-catching (and contentious) feature of the Paramount design was a short 'feature' window, intended to separate the main side windows from the first bay, which had its lower edge sloping down toward the front, with a break in the waist trim below the short window.

The 3200 continued the first bay's slope through the lower edges of the driver's and passenger-door windows, which then aligned with the base of the single-piece curved windscreen. The 3500 had deeper driver's and passenger-door windows with straight lower edges that aligned with that model's deeper, horizontally divided two-piece windscreen. The divide continued the line of the passenger door's top edge, above which was a small window.

Twin radial-arm windscreen wipers could be specified instead of standard pantograph units. Operators requiring a Paramount 3200 conforming to the Bus Grant specification or fitted with destination equipment received theirs equipped with a three-piece windscreen. The destination display was located above a horizontal divide, with pantograph wipers for the vertically divided lower screens.

A black plastic panel was set in the dash above a bright metal grille and headlamp surround, within which single

**Coopers of Killamarsh entered this immaculate Leyland Tiger with Mk I Paramount 3500 body in the 2003 Brighton Coach Rally. The waist trim ceases beneath the feature window as on the Mk I 3200 but does not continue beneath the windscreen or driver's cab and passenger-door windows, unlike the 3200. A plug door is fitted — the hidden lower step edge is the clue.**

**For the Paramount range Plaxton offered a variety of standard livery layouts, many of which were adopted by operators.** courtesy R. E. GRAY

rectangular headlamps with adjoining indicator units were fitted. The Paramount's rear end was taken almost directly from the Supreme V and VI but with a deeper illuminated panel and rear window.

Plaxton developed a range of standard specification packages for the Paramount. The initial star-rated coach plan offered upgrades from the standard specification from one to four stars. The standard specification included items such as electric windscreen wipers, ducted heating, an air-powered plug door on the 3500, rear Continental door and steps on the 3500, and Smiths Radiomobile radio and public-address system.

A single star added, for example, stainless-steel wheel discs, roof insulation, a Smiths Radio Cassette and a Paramount Design Schemes livery layout, chosen from the 10 available. Two stars gave the operator the one-star option plus the likes of reclining seats, fog and spot lamps, maximum underfloor sound insulation (one wonders what the minimum was), Blaupunkt radio, public-address and stereo-cassette system and tinted side windows.

Another star was added to gain double-glazed side windows, Tempo 100 specification (which allowed approved coaches to travel at 100km/h on Germany's motorways), and a plug-type entrance door (for the 3200). Top of the range four-star models could boast a toilet and washroom (sunken or at saloon height), carpet or moquette trim on the interior side panels, and — for the 3200 — a waist-height Continental door. Other options were available for operators which required different feature combinations from those packaged together by Plaxton.

The Paramount 3200 was initially available in 8m, 10m, 11m and 12m lengths, with standard seating capacities of 35, 45, 53 and 57 respectively; the Paramount 3500 was available in just 11m and 12m lengths. A basic 12m 3500 body when launched cost £35,985, the four-star package leaving a £49,145-sized dent in the purchaser's pocket.

The 11m and 12m Paramounts were fitted with four window bays aft of the feature window — the first of these being noticeably shorter on the 11m variant — with the rear offside bay equally divided by the emergency door. The 10m 3200 had three window bays aft of the feature window with the rear offside divided as before. The short 8m version omitted the feature window to accommodate two and a half bays aft of the sloping first bay, the emergency door fitting into the offside rear half-bay.

The 3200 was available on chassis from Bedford, DAF, Dennis, Ford, Leyland, Scania, Ward Bros and Volvo, whereas the heavier 3500 required heavy-duty chassis from DAF, Dennis, Leyland, Scania or Volvo. Other chassis manufacturers would be added through the Paramount's production life.

*Above:* **Mervyn's of Innesdown operated this 1984 Bedford YMP with Mk I Paramount 3200 body for a number of years on its Hampshire County Council-contracted bus service from Winchester to Micheldever. The coach is seen at the entrance to Mervyn's base in March 1998. The 10m Paramount can be identified by three standard-length bays aft of the feature window.**

*Below:* **Taylor of Sutton Scotney operated this 1986 Ford R1115 with Mk I Paramount 3200 35-seat bodywork, which had been new to Weller of Midhurst. It is seen in Southampton in October 1990. The 8m Paramount 3200 lacked the short feature window in the second bay to reduce the proliferation of uprights that would otherwise result. The emergency exit fitted neatly into the resulting rear half-bay. Note the use of wheel trims originally developed for the 4000.**

Paramount 4000

The Paramount 4000 is the third luxury coach in the new generation of Plaxtons coaches. Scheduled for introduction late 1983, the 4000 combines the elegance and style of the 3000 series with an intelligently designed twin deck body, which maximises both passenger accommodation, and locker capacities.
The twin configuration however, can also offer adaptability with many potential interior layout options being possible.
This will of course make it equally at home on both long haul motorway express routes and important Executive operations with its ability to offer high seating capacities or alternatively superb Executive layouts.
Adaptability will be further increased with capabilities to meet current British and European including Tempo 100 regulations enabling the vehicle to be equally successful on Continental operations.
But, whilst being an enormously practical design, this magnificent coach will inevitably be one of the most impressive vehicles in any fleet. Passengers will be certain to appreciate its comfort and good looks ensuring the popularity of both the coach and its operator with its prestigious image.



*Right:* **The artist's impression of the Paramount 4000 – Plaxton's first double-deck model – didn't do justice to the finished article.** ***courtesy R. E. Gray***

*Below:* **South Wales operated this 1986 Mk II Paramount 4000 based on a Neoplan N722/3 underframe. It was a 71-seater with toilet.**

The Paramount quickly proved a popular choice for operators of all sizes across the length and breadth of the UK, from National Bus Company fleets to small independents with a handful of vehicles.

Excelsior of Bournemouth had operated several generations of Plaxton-bodied Ford coaches so found itself able to specify a significant revision to the Paramount body when placing its first order. Two DAF SB2300 and 21 Ford R1115 were delivered in the spring of 1983 without the feature window, thereby enabling the use of four standard-length bays on the 11m vehicles.

Plaxton built its first coaches with low driving positions for Excelsior in 1984, on the Quest 80 VM. This was a rear-engined 12m chassis with major mechanical parts common to the Ford Cargo truck range. The special variant of the Paramount 3200 body had a lowered front end to make best use of the Quest chassis' low driving position. The deeper windscreen and driver's window of the 3500 were fitted, and the feature window was omitted, in common with Excelsior's previous Paramount deliveries. A total of 25 were ordered, but trouble with the initial deliveries saw just 17 supplied. The last was destroyed by fire in the month following delivery, and four other chassis were used by Excelsior for spares. The 16 survivors were sold prior to the 1986 season, although at the time of writing one remains in PCV service as part of The Running Footman fleet.

A model of a double-deck coach had been displayed by Plaxton at the 1982 Motor Show, and the prototype was launched in January 1984 as the Paramount 4000, the figure once again representing the overall height in millimetres. It was based upon a three-axle Neoplan N722/3 underframe powered by a Mercedes-Benz OM422 V10 engine, the Neoplan being chosen as a proven product that saved Plaxton the expense of developing its own underframe. The Neoplan frame extended to the underside of the lower-deck windows, Plaxton building the remaining structure using a number of standard Paramount parts.

The Paramount 4000 bore a close family resemblance to the single-deck 3200 and 3500 — the front grille assembly and rear lights were identical, and much similarity of styling was in evidence elsewhere. But significantly the 4000 lacked the feature window and was fitted with bonded side glazing, with just the front windscreens being rubber mounted. The 4000 was also offered with a range of specification packages from the standard one star (featuring 83 fixed seats, wheels discs of a new design and tinted windows) to four stars (full bar service, video and five colour monitors, courier call and intercom system and hostess seat). Thirty Neoplan-based Paramount 4000 coaches were constructed in the period 1984-6. The prototype was sold to Excelsior of Bournemouth and exhibited at the 1984 Motor Show, a 12-week strike at Plaxton frustrating plans to exhibit the 1985 range.

Plaxton's 1985 Paramount was launched in the January of that year. The revised, Mk II range comprised six basic models, the existing 3200, 3500 and 4000 being joined by the 3200LS, 3500LS and 4000RS. The two LS models had lowered driving positions using conversions of DAF, Leyland, Scania and Volvo chassis to give a similar look to Excelsior's Quest 80 VMs. Both LS variants featured deep two-piece windscreens, that on the 3200LS identical to that of the standard 3500, whilst that of the 3500LS was even deeper.

The 4000RS used the 4000 structure fitted to the mid-engined Volvo B10MT chassis. A rear saloon was fitted behind the rear axle beneath a full-length upper deck, and a massive (13.4cu m) luggage space was provided amidships in an underfloor bay. Newton of Dingwall received the first two examples, in April 1985. A further 21 were built up to 1990, Flights of Birmingham taking 18 of these for its network of airport services, on which the large luggage capacity could be put to good use.

The extended range was matched by a number of revised features. The Mk II Paramount had a modified interior with soft trim throughout and with new parcel racks that could accommodate air-conditioning. Bonded glazing became a no-cost option, and full-length waist trim now bridged the gap left beneath the feature window on the Mk I. The plastic wheel trims developed for the 4000 were made available across the range, the same material now being used for a neater grille and headlamp surround that lacked the previous fluted black panel above it. The 3200 driver's cab and passenger-door windows lost their lower edge slopes to align fully with the windscreen, leaving a step up to the saloon glazing.

Availability of the 4000 was extended during 1985 to the rear-engined Scania K112 chassis, the first two being delivered in December to Grey-Green of London and Harris of Thurrock. Twenty more were built on the K112 and successor K113 between 1986 and 1990.

The Paramount Mk II range was to remain in production for a relatively short period. Its Ogle-styled Mk III successor was launched at the 1986 Motor Show and featured a new aerodynamic front end. The windscreens of the new 3200 and 3500 were both horizontally divided with the upper section tilted back. A new front panel featured a restyled centre grille. Impact-resistant bumpers abutted the headlamp and grille assembly or encompassed just the fog-light and lower grille area, depending on the operator's chosen option.

The most recognisable change was the loss of the feature window and sloping first bay. Instead a window the shape of an irregular pentagon was provided immediately aft of the driver's cab and passenger door on all but the shortest 8m variant. Bonded windows were now standard. The Paramount 4000 was not updated to Mk III specification until the 1989 season but was offered from 1987 in its Mk II form on the DAF SBR3000 chassis. A total of 24 were built over three years, Park's of Hamilton receiving the first, in March 1987.

**A London Country North West Leyland Tiger in Jetlink 747 livery leaves Heathrow Terminal 4 bus station in August 1989. The coach was new in 1985 and carries Mk II 3500LS bodywork — the LS (Low Screen) designation identifying the low driving position and resulting deeper lower windscreen (the upper section is identical to that on the standard 3500). Note how the lower edges of the windscreen and driver's window fall beneath the lower waist moulding's alignment. Bonded glazing is fitted, and the trim beneath the windows lacks a bright insert. An offside Continental door is fitted aft of the rear axle in place of a conventional emergency exit at saloon-floor level.**

*Above:* **A 1986 Southdown Leyland Tiger with a Mk II Paramount 3200 body loads in Commercial Road, Portsmouth, in May 1989 while operating on the 727 Portsmouth–Southampton express service. The 12m body can be identified by the longer third bay immediately aft of the short feature window. On the Mk II 3200 the waist trim was continued beneath the feature window but did not continue forward of the first bay — the lower edge of the driver's cab window (and, on the nearside, the passenger-door window) aligning with that of the windscreen. The Mk II body can also be identified by the narrow black surround to the front dash panel.**

*Below:* **Elcock Reisen of Telford operated this Volvo B10M with Mk II Paramount 3500 bodywork, which had been new in 1986 to Clarke of London. It is seen in a Bath coach park in 1992. Bonded glazing is fitted, and the feature window omitted — both options on the Mk II Paramount.**

**In 1988 Shamrock & Rambler took four Leyland Tigers with Mk III Paramount 3200 48-seat bodywork, one of which is seen on layover at The Hard Interchange, Portsmouth, soon after delivery. The Mk III bodywork can be identified by the style of front grille fitted and the pentagon-shaped first window bay. It is fitted with a three-piece windscreen to accommodate destination equipment, and has a one-piece swing entrance door. The optional front bumper reaches to the underside of the headlamp/grille assembly on this vehicle. Lower rubbing strips are carried only on the rear panels at bumper level.**

Odd Paramounts in 1987 were four used to rebody 10-year-old Leyland Leopard chassis for Wallace Arnold. Nothing unusual in that, you might think, as a number of chassis received replacement Paramount bodies over the years. But these were 10m long and just 7ft 8½in wide — instead of the standard 2.5m (8ft 2½in) — for West Country operations.

Plaxton, its Kirkby Coach & Bus associate and Volvo worked with National Express to develop a standard specification coach to raise service quality. The Expressliner was based on the three-star Paramount 3500 mounted on a Volvo B10M Mk III chassis, the package being formally launched in March 1989. Two Expressliner variants were available — 44- or 46-seat 'Rapide' vehicles with a galley unit, and 47- or 49-seat conventional vehicles without. The rear window was replaced by a full-depth panel embossed with a large double-N symbol. Luggage lockers were fitted, with parallel lift doors to facilitate loading in confined areas, and doors were also fitted to the sides of the boot in place of a conventional rear lid. The vehicles were leased by operators from National Expressliners, a joint venture between Plaxton and the National Westminster Bank, deals being linked to National Express operating contracts. The first Expressliners entered service in March 1989, when two of National Express's own fleet of eight, with distinctive NXI registrations, appeared on the London–Bristol and London–Liverpool routes.

Plaxton announced in 1991 that its single-deck Paramount range was to be replaced before the year's end by its new Premiere and Excalibur models. The Paramount 4000 was to remain in production

**Barnes of Aldbourne owned this 1989 DAF SB2300 with Mk III Paramount 3200LS bodywork with low driving position. The dash panel is similar to that used on the Mk III Paramount 4000. A single-piece swing door is fitted, as the lower step edge is visible.**

*Left:* **In 1990 Dorset Travel Services received five Volvo B10Ms with Mk III Paramount 3500 bodies to Expressliner specification. One loads at The Hard Interchange, Portsmouth in 1992. The lower windscreen is divided vertically, and an optional front bumper fitted that reaches partway to the grille/headlight panel. A lower locker door may be spotted forward of the rear emergency exit — this provided boot access, as the Expressliner was built without a rear boot lid.**

*Right:* **A Cambridge Coach Services Volvo B10M with Mk III Paramount 3500 bodywork, new in 1990 to Park's of Hamilton, calls at Gorleston-on-Sea, Suffolk, in September 1997. The body has a rear emergency door at saloon-floor level and a centre Continental door.**

*Left:* **At the 2001 Brighton Coach Rally Chivers of Wallington entered this 1987 Mk III Paramount 3200-bodied DAF SB2300, which had been new to Dore of Leafield, Oxfordshire. It is fitted with the deeper front bumper, extending to the lower edge of the headlight/grille panel.**

because development costs for a new double-deck coach model could not be justified on financial grounds, although it turned out that no more were built. Plaxton did, however, build a final batch of Paramount 3500 bodies on DAF MB230 chassis in 1992 to aid Bus Éireann's fleet standardisation.

Many Paramounts remain in service. Examples of the 3200, 3500 and 4000 in Mk I, Mk II and Mk III forms may still be sighted, albeit in steadily decreasing numbers as the effects of age are felt. Care is often required in identifying different types as a number of older Paramounts received updated body parts during their service lives; for instance, Mk III dash panels may be found on Mk I or II examples. A small number can also be spied on the rally field in preservation.

Was the Paramount of paramount importance? To answer that question one need only look at the contrast in fortunes between Plaxton and its then major UK competitor, Duple, since 1982, when both introduced new ranges to the UK coach market. From where would the UK have sourced its coach bodywork if the Paramount had failed, and Plaxton disappeared in Duple fashion?

*Above:* **Delivered new to Harrod's Coaches of Wormegay, Norfolk, in 1989 was this Dennis Javelin with Mk III Paramount 3200 body, seen at Showbus 2008. It carries the larger bumper fitting and the standard two-piece windscreen fitted to the Mk III 3200.**

*Left:* **Rambler of St Leonards-on-Sea refurbished this ex-Wallace Arnold 1991 Volvo B10M with Mk III Paramount 3500 body, fitting a new dash panel and chrome moulding. It is seen at the 2007 Cobham Bus Museum's Longcross rally and running day.**

# Grand National

It was, perhaps, the Marmite of buses — you either loved it or loathed it. Either way, the Leyland National could be found in a diverse range of environments, as **Chris Drew** observes.

*Left:* **Pennine Way. Making its way along the stunning Aire Valley, a Pennine Motors National heads for Settle at the end of the working day.**

*Below:* **Worcester Porcelain. A Midland Red National coming off the bridge in Worcester on a particularly wet day in the summer of 1974. In the background is the Cathedral, where it is possible to climb to the top of the tower and survey the area — and use it as a platform to photograph the local buses.**

*Left:* **Bath Night. The third floor of a multi-storey car park in Bath was an idea vantage point for this view of a Bristol Omnibus National. The driver turned off his engine and all went silent — and click, this was the result.**

*Below:* **Ain't No Oil Painting. Surely not the most glamorous way to arrive at a stately home, but at least arrive one could without a car. The grounds of Chartwell House act as a backdrop for a London Country National which was among the least luxurious of vehicles to bear the Green Line name.**

*Right:* **Fleetwood Mac. Under the lighthouse, under the tram wires and all under blue skies at Fleetwood. A pair of Ribble Nationals murmur quietly to each other whilst waiting to run out on a couple of local services.**

*Below:* **Show Pony. In the early 1970s Leyland Nationals were appearing at motor shows all over the place. Slightly out of the ordinary, this National, known as the Lifeliner, was exhibited at the 1974 Earl's Court show. Fitted out as a mobile casualty and communications centre to be used at the site of a major incident, it had space for masses of equipment, including six beds with monitoring facilities and an inflatable boat. This vehicle was later converted to an ordinary bus and ended up with Midland Red.**

*Above:* **Herd of Jumbos. Small fleets of articulated buses appeared in Sheffield and at Heathrow Airport in the late 1970s. 1979 saw the entry into service in Sheffield of five DAB chassis with bodywork made up of standard National parts at Workington. It was a very clever adaptation, because the DAB chassis had an underfloor engine, so the floor level was higher than that of a National. The second DAB artic order, for seven vehicles for British Airways, was put together at the Charles H. Roe factory in Leeds and featured five doors with room for a total capacity of 145, with 100 standing. One is seen on the apron at Heathrow in the company of British Airways Lockheed Tristar G-BECC *The English Miss Rose.* Nowadays security restrictions stop people taking photographs from the top couple of floors of airport car parks. Such is life!**

*Left:* **Back to Front. The National 2 had its radiator moved forward to make space for the 680 engine, which was bigger than the 500 it replaced. This National, new to Nottingham City Transport, is seen leaving Stamford bus station in the ownership of Road Car, once better known as the Lincolnshire Road Car Co.**

# Madder and yet madder still

**Gavin Booth** examines the Renilson years, a period of transformation at Lothian Buses.

*All photographs by the author.*

### The man

Neil Renilson was Chief Executive of Lothian Buses from 1999 to the start of 2009 and oversaw an amazing transformation of a respected but conservative bus company.

He came to Lothian with an excellent pedigree. He started with Edinburgh Corporation in 1971 and then moved to Loughborough University where he gained a BSc in Transport Management and Planning. He then joined the National Bus Company's legendary senior-management training scheme, progressing through a raft of companies before arriving at Northern General, where he was Operations Manager during NBC's privatisation. Then came a chance to move back to Scotland as Managing Director of the Scottish Bus Group's Strathtay company, before two years later moving to join the fledgling Stagecoach operation, where he stayed for 10 years as a valued lieutenant to founders Brian Souter and Ann Gloag.

**Neil Renilson, wearing one of his trademark sports jackets.**

He says: "I learned a lot at NBC, who did a pretty good job considering the constraints they were under. SBG was different — there I learned how *not* to do things. Then I was involved in the early days at Stagecoach, which were very exciting. I learned a huge amount from those times, and I wouldn't have missed them for the world. Brian and Ann were wonderful people to work with, and I have an immense respect for them. And at Northern I worked with Martin Ballinger and Chris Moyes – and with Brian King and Ian Morgan at Trent; I was lucky that I landed in companies with great people at the helm and who have since turned out to be major figures in the bus industry. I had excellent tutors all along the way."

And, arriving at Lothian with the previous team all approaching retirement age, Neil was able to hand-pick his own senior team, who have all contributed greatly to Lothian's success. Before he left Lothian in 2009 Neil was asked to sum up his decade at the helm: "In this industry, the acid test is 'Are you leaving the company in a better state than you found it?'; well, with passenger numbers up from 82 million to 114 million, a fleet average age of 5 years and record profitability, I believe I am."

### The challenge

It takes Edinburgh people a long time to adapt to new names. Although the name hasn't been used for a long time, Edinburgh's other main bus operator, First Edinburgh, is still regularly called 'SMT' by locals, and people even talk about 'the green buses', even though green doesn't feature in the Barbie palette.

And so it was with Lothian. Although the operation morphed from Edinburgh Corporation Transport to Lothian Region Transport in 1975, the initials 'LRT' are still popularly used for buses in spite of the name-change to Lothian Buses plc in 2000.

The name-change may have been an attempt to shake off LRT's image as a highly competent but staid and slightly stuffy operator that was more than a little old-fashioned. LRT had firmly seen off much of the initial sparring from Eastern Scottish that followed deregulation in 1986, but with an increasingly complex route network and a complicated fare structure, it was looking just a bit tired and vulnerable to attack. Its new double-deck buses since 1982 had all been long-wheelbase Leyland and Volvo Olympians, efficient but unexciting in their traditional livery with antiseptic grey interiors and red vinyl-covered seats. The interiors had, Neil said, "all the allure of a hospital corridor. They were always scrupulously clean and smelt of carbolic soap, but they certainly weren't warm and welcoming."

Although LRT had kept First at bay it had come dangerously close to allowing Arriva into Edinburgh on tendered services, which could have seriously undermined Lothian's previously undisputed position as Edinburgh's principal bus operator. LRT needed a makeover, and Neil wasted no time in getting to grips with the route network, the fares, the fleet, the garages — the whole business, in fact.

### The network

The tram and bus network that Edinburgh Corporation had developed covered the city comprehensively, most bus services beyond the city boundary being worked by SMT (later Scottish Omnibuses, Eastern Scottish and predecessor of today's First Edinburgh). As Lothian Region Transport the city operator made token excursions across the boundary until deregulation in 1986, when the gloves were definitely off. Just as Eastern Scottish launched a network of services in Edinburgh, Lothian struck out into East Lothian, Midlothian and West Lothian. For many people living beyond the Edinburgh boundary it seemed natural that buses labelled 'Lothian' should serve them, and part of the attraction was that Lothian's fares were perceived as cheaper than Eastern's; previously fares on Eastern Scottish services had risen sharply once the city boundary was crossed.

As is often the case, it is easier for a city operator to expand outwards, perhaps with only a couple of extra buses in the cycle, than for the out-of-town operator to mount a challenge from outside. And so it proved as some of the less profitable Eastern routes dropped away, while Lothian increased its presence in the adjoining areas.

By something approaching coincidence, Lothian withdrew from West Lothian and South Queensferry at around the same time as Eastern decided to withdraw from some city services, including what was possibly its most successful, the C5 minibus.

So the network inherited by Neil and his team provided comprehensive coverage of the city and a significant presence to the east and south. The Eastern Scottish routes (now First Edinburgh) all operated beyond the city boundaries, with duplication on the main corridors into Edinburgh — as indeed there always had been — with only one route that really competed directly with Lothian, the cross-city 44 between Wallyford and Balerno. Lothian's route, the long-established 44, had grown at each end with deregulation, while the First 44 was a combination of two routes that had previously terminated in the centre of Edinburgh.

A look at the 1999 Lothian network revealed that it had grown messy and complicated, with confusing new route numbers and a plague of route-number suffixes. Comparing the 1999 Lothian route map with the older Edinburgh Corporation maps that adorned the company's boardroom showed how much routes had strayed from the simpler and more sensible network that had existed 40 or so years previously.

Of course, the city had changed in the 40-odd years since the first-generation trams had been replaced, but some routes were serving areas that no longer needed intensive services, while newer traffic generators like suburban shopping centres were under-provided.

The outcome in March 2000 was the largest package of route revisions ever implemented at one time. New connections were made, new termini established, old route

**Lothian's first long-wheelbase Leyland Olympians were ECW-bodied and delivered between 1982 and 1986. One of the significant changes following the March 2000 service changes was the routeing of the 1 service, Edinburgh Corporation's first bus route in 1919, along Princes Street, as seen here, rather than the Royal Mile.**

numbers reinstated — and while it was always unlikely that such a major change would go 100% smoothly, it laid the foundations for Lothian's subsequent success. There would be tweaks where things didn't work out quite as planned, or to reflect a fast-changing city.

High-frequency services were identified, running up to every five minutes during working hours, and these would soon be route-branded. One was the long cross-city 26 route, which increased Lothian's presence in East Lothian, and the 22, where a solid long-standing double-deck service was transformed into a high-frequency single-deck route, using the West Approach Road, built on former railway trackbed. This provided a fast service to the west, bypassing inner-suburban congestion, and establishing termini at two important shopping centres.

*Above:* **Reworking the 22, converting a double-deck route into a high-frequency single-deck route, was one of Neil Renilson's early successes at Lothian. It started with Dennis/Plaxton Darts like this one in Princes Street in 2000, before moving on to heavier Volvo/Wright single-deckers – and in 2009 to double-deckers.**

The 22 and 26 were probably the most visible signs of the new regime, and much of the success of the 22 was the decision to single-deck the route; previously Lothian had been very much a double-deck operator, with single-deckers used only on lightly-loaded or low bridge routes. In 1999 less than 10% of the Lothian fleet was single-deck; in 2009 it was over 20%. By the time Neil Renilson retired from Lothian in 2009 the company had an established strong presence in East Lothian, and a stronger presence in Midlothian, where it had become the main operator.

He also tackled night buses. Where there had been six routes that bore no relationship to daytime services, the services were totally reworked into a proper network, all very similar to daytime routes, carrying those route numbers but with 'N' prefixes, and running seven nights a week.

Another aspect of Lothian's operations was the fare structure. In 1999 there were six adult single fares ranging from 50p for the shortest trip to £1.60 for trips beyond the city. The fares were difficult to understand and open to abuse, so Neil decided to go for a flat fare, something that few UK city operators had tried. Over a few years the fare structure was simplified, culminating in a move to a £1 adult fare, with extremely popular day tickets and a hard sell on Ridacard season tickets, which from 2000 moved to smartcard technology. Against the background of an increasing proportion of non-cash transactions, the flat-fare move was a success, and, to speed boarding, pavement-mounted ticket machines at busy stops give passengers the chance to buy single and day tickets before they board a bus.

*Right:* **The first purpose-built permanent open-top double-deckers for the UK for some 60 years were four Dennis Trident/Plaxton Presidents delivered to Lothian in 2000. They originally wore this tartan version of the Edinburgh Classic Tour livery but soon reappeared in red City Sightseeing colours.**

***Left:*** **Several of the buses acquired with the former Guide Friday business in 2002 were retained by Lothian. This Leyland Olympian/Roe was new in 1984 to London Country and is seen turning from the Lawnmarket into Bank Street in 2003, wearing the lighter-green version of Guide Friday livery adopted by Lothian.**

***Below:*** **The Mac Tours operation is run by former London Routemasters, now principally the 10 extra-long ERMs, like this part-open-top example seen at Holyrood in June 2004.**

## The tours

Edinburgh has long been an important tourist destination, and tours of the city had been pioneered by Edinburgh Corporation in its earliest motor-bus days. These were traditional guided tours of the main city sights using single-deck coaches, and by the 1990s the tour programme also included longer day tours around Scotland and extended tours in the UK and overseas. A conventional tour fleet was maintained, mainly Leyland Tigers and Dennis Javelins, and there were a couple of open-top double-deckers that were not really used extensively. Then Guide Friday moved into Edinburgh with open-toppers, prompting Lothian to rush a handful of its older Leyland Atlanteans into its workshops for conversion to open-top. Guide Friday responded by challenging Lothian on the Airport service.

This was the scenario Neil inherited. It soon became clear that the traditional coach-tour fleet was on its way out; as many other bus companies discovered, while it might be a bit of a diversion running coaches, the staff effort was not matched by the revenue. Open-toppers, on the other hand, were potential money-spinners. An early indication of this was the purchase of four new open-top Dennis Tridents, the first new open-toppers for a UK operator for 60 years, and the upgrading of the existing open-top fleet, moving from Atlanteans to Olympians.

There was also the question of Guide Friday, but the demise of that company led to Lothian's taking over the Guide Friday tours, and Lothian also signed up to the City Sightseeing franchise, introducing the striking red livery to the tours fleet, alongside the former Guide Friday tours, now running in a revised light green and cream. Then another competitor, locally based Mac Tours, arrived on the scene, majoring on vintage tours with a mixed fleet that included Bristol Lodekkas and front-engined Leyland Titans. When Lothian acquired the Mac Tours business in 2002 the fleet also included former London Routemasters that had been bought with a view to conversion for open-top tours. These formed the basis of the continuing Mac Tours operation under Lothian control, and Lothian went on to build up a fleet of 20 Routemasters, including virtually every variant – RM, RML, RMC, RMA, RCL and all 10 of the lengthened ERMs. As with the other Lothian tour brands the Routemasters were a mix of open-top, partly open-top and even closed-top buses. The Routemaster fleet was reduced in 2009 when the ERMs became the standard Mac Tours fare.

Some of the earliest closed-top Dennis Tridents were converted for the City Sightseeing tour and later the green-liveried Edinburgh Tour. And a fourth brand was added — the blue/yellow Majestic Tour, taking in the former Royal Yacht *Britannia* at Leith. Today the tours run all year, something that 20 years ago would have seemed unlikely with open-toppers, given the Edinburgh climate. And they offer visitors a choice of live and guided commentaries, low-floor or vintage buses, and a chance to see the tourist beat or explore more of the city.

The Lothian open-top-tour operation is the largest outside London, carrying around half-a-million passengers in a year, and regularly ranks among the top three paid-for tourist attractions in Scotland.

*Above:* **The harlequin livery was introduced with the launch of the first low-floor buses for the Lothian fleet in 1999, the five Dennis Tridents with low-height Alexander ALX400 bodies. Note the madder skirt and wheels and the gold and red diamonds, the branding for the 44 route and the blue moquette seats.**

*Below:* **In an effort to find better-wearing paints Lothian tried a lighter red on a handful of buses. This 1988 Leyland Olympian/Alexander RH in Princes Street in 2004 demonstrates the white-on-black roller blinds that Lothian, almost uniquely among large operators, prefers to yellow lettering or electronic displays.**

## The livery

There was much wailing and gnashing of teeth when Neil Renilson changed the traditional Lothian livery. Some who were unhappy with the move even demanded Neil's resignation. Yes, really.

Since time began — well, certainly for more than a century — Edinburgh's municipal trams and buses had been painted madder and white. In 1999 the main Lothian bus fleet was still painted in these colours, complete with a bit of gold lining-out. The buses looked uniform and traditional and, frankly, dull. Madder looks great in bright sunshine when buses emerge from the paintshop but very quickly loses its gloss and on a dull day can look flat and unappealing.

With the first low-floor buses due in 1999, pre-Renilson Lothian had looked at liveries, and visuals I have seen reveal designs that would have looked heavy and overbearing. The scheme that appeared on the first low-floor double-deckers was not one for the traditionalists but made sure that low-floor buses stood out from the rest. The madder content was greatly reduced — just the skirt and the wheels — with the rest largely white but with a striking red and gold diamond theme; they quickly became the 'harlequins', and while this livery was refined over the years it remained the generic fleet scheme.

The next development was route-branding, initially with colour-coded vinyls below the upper deck windows, which in 2004 grew to distinctively-coloured top decks that helped passengers to identify their buses from a distance. Later, single-deckers on main routes were route-branded with coloured roofs.

One of the problems with madder — a non-standard 'special mix' colour — was achieving consistency of colour from one batch to the next, so Lothian tried some similar but standard shades, but reverted to madder for the Olympian fleet. The red shade used on the harlequins was used to route-brand the Olympians on the 15 service.

The Olympians for the Airport service had worn their own distinctive blue livery, and when Lothian introduced a policy of regularly updating its airport fleet this was adapted to the new generation low-floor buses used on the service. In 2010 it was replaced by a new but still blue-based livery.

In 2010 Lothian introduced an updated version of the madder-and-white livery, with gold relief, this being applied initially to Wright-bodied Volvos, with coloured tops for route-branded services.

## The fleet

There was nothing intrinsically wrong with the Lothian fleet at the start of 1999. The double-deckers were mainly Leyland and Volvo Olympians with ECW or Alexander bodies; the newest, delivered in 1997, had Alexander Royale bodies. All but one prototype were long-wheelbase buses, the vast majority with separate entrance and exit doors, with seats for up to 83 passengers to cope with the

**The blue Airlink livery, at first applied to Olympians, was adapted for low-floor buses – initially successive batches of Plaxton President-bodied Dennis Tridents, like this 2001 delivery, seen in 2004 passing the new Edinburgh Bus Station in St Andrew Square and, unusually, operating on a normal bus service.**

**The first serious route branding was introduced on the new fleet of 11.4m-long Trident/Presidents introduced in 2004. These used a red and gold scheme, but still with madder skirt and wheels.**

crowds. Single-deckers were very much in the minority. There were 20 Leyland Nationals, 12 Leyland Lynxes and 12 step-entrance Dennis Darts.

The first low-floor double-deckers had been ordered before Neil Renilson's appointment, a toe-in-the-water order for 15 Dennis Tridents (five with Alexander ALX400 bodies, the rest Plaxton Presidents) and six Volvo B7TL/Presidents. The first of these, the Trident/Alexanders, arrived in 1999, though the bodybuilder had insisted on providing buses to Stagecoach London specification — low-height buses with an awkwardly-placed exit door — which meant they never really fitted into the fleet and within 10 years had become open-top tour buses.

The Plaxton President versions proved to be a happier buy, and Lothian would stay with Plaxton right to the end of production at Wigan. Experience of the early Tridents led to improvements on each successive batch. The exit door moved forward on the later 2000 deliveries, and from 2002 Lothian turned to even longer buses.

What the Tridents did introduce to Lothian was — gasp — moquette seating, initially on traditional bus seats, but Lothian quickly moved to modular seats. The first moquette was a pale blue, but a striking tartan — the official 'Edinburgh Tartan' — was quickly adopted as standard.

Since 1969 most of Edinburgh's buses had been of dual-door layout, and unlike most operators it had stuck with a separate exit door in the interests of fast loading at busy city-centre stops. But concerns about safety and fraudulent insurance claims forced Lothian in 2002 to revert to single-door double-deckers. All deliveries since that time have been single-door buses, and Lothian subsequently removed the exit doors from many of the earlier Tridents and the B7TLs.

Lothian's early low-floor double-deckers had been 10.5m long, but the Tridents delivered from 2002 were 11.4m long, with seats for up to 83 passengers, to provide a seating capacity similar to that of the long Olympians. The technical specification was improved with more powerful engines and a move to Voith gearboxes. Edinburgh is a hilly city, and the first Tridents had found the hills a bit of a challenge.

One of the big changes at Lothian was a move to increase the number of single-deck buses in the fleet. So the inherited Nationals, Lynxes and Darts were joined by low-floor Dennis/Plaxton Super Pointer Darts, 90 of them between 2000 and 2003, and, when a need for heavier-weight single-deckers was identified, by Volvo B7RLEs with Wright Eclipse bodies, 70 between 2004 and 2009. Smaller single-deckers had never really figured in the Lothian fleet — no minibuses (except for a couple of ex-Stagecoach examples for the Mac Tours fleet) and just 12 step-entrance Dennis Dart/Alexander Dash midibuses, which were never fully utilised. These were all sold during the Renilson years but were replaced for contracted Lothian and Mac Tours services with six Optare Solo SRs bought in 2008.

Second-hand buses rarely figured in the Edinburgh city fleet, yet in 2001 Lothian invested in 17 Volvo-engined Mk 1 Leyland Nationals from a variety of sources as a stopgap and low-cost method of maintaining the fleet size during First's competitive attack. Once First had withdrawn to lick its wounds, these Nationals were sold in 2003. Another second-hand investment was a Volvo B7TL/Plaxton President demonstrator that had been built largely to Lothian specification and which fitted well with Lothian's own six examples.

With the Plaxton President body no longer available, Lothian was looking for a new source of double-decks and settled for the Volvo B7TL with 11.4m-long Wright Gemini body, following successful experience with the Volvo/Wright single-deckers. Since 2005 it has placed 300 B7TLs and B9TLs in service. Lothian's only move away from Dennis or Volvo double-deckers has been investment in 15 Scania OmniCitys for the Airlink service in 2006/7. The high-frequency Airlink service between the city centre and the airport had been regularly updated with new Tridents with extra luggage space and tables, which were cascaded to normal bus duties when replacements arrived. But from 2007 the entire Airlink service was run by the Scanias, though these were themselves replaced in 2010 by new Volvo/Wrights. The Scanias introduced a more upmarket feel to the Airlink fleet, with leather coach-type seats, and this quality is maintained on the new Volvos.

**From 2005 the Volvo B7TL with Wright Gemini single-door bodywork became the Lothian standard, some being delivered in fleet colours and others, as here, in route-branded livery. A 2006 delivery, branded for the 44, is seen in Musselburgh, with the Firth of Forth and the hills of Fife in the background.**

*Right:* **In 2006/7 Lothian bought 15 Scania OmniCity double-deckers for the Airlink service. This one is climbing The Mound, with the National Gallery of Scotland in the background.**

*Below:* **This Volvo B7LA with Hispano bodywork was tried on a couple of Lothian routes, with Lothian vinyls added to its London red livery. It is pictured at Haymarket in 2005 on a short-working of the 26 route.**

Scania also provided Lothian with a demonstrator on long-term loan, a 90-seat N94/East Lancs OmniDekka, similar to extra-long-wheelbase buses built for Nottingham City Transport. A Volvo B7L/Hispano articulated bus was also supplied on long-term loan, but this, like the OmniDekka, was not retained. Lothian did buy a former Scania OmniCity artic demonstrator in 2008, but this had a short life in the fleet, working on park-and-ride services.

## The tram

Proposals for trams and guided buses in Edinburgh were always around from the 1980s, but none had come to anything. The £50 million CERT — City of Edinburgh Rapid Transit — project proposed a network of guided busways between the city centre and the airport. The biggest bus groups submitted joint bids as part of consortia, and ConCERT (which included FirstGroup) was successful, but by early 2001 it had pulled out, stating that the project was no longer viable and blaming improved Lothian bus services along the route.

To test the concept the city built what was at the time the UK's longest continuous stretch of guided busway, linking the Saughton and Broomhouse areas to the west of the city, avoiding two busy junctions with overbridges. The 1.5km £10 million Edinburgh Fastlink busway system opened in 2004 and was used by guidewheel-fitted buses on Lothian's high-frequency 22 route and the double-deck 2 route.

But also on the horizon was a major tramway scheme with proposals for a network of lines, and even though its future was in doubt for some time, construction work started in 2006 with a target opening date of 2011 —

though 2013 now seems more likely. The original 27-mile network was pared down to a single 11-mile route from the airport to the city centre (like the stillborn CERT project) and then to Leith and Newhaven — in essence, said the critics, spending £550 million to replace the 22 bus with the 22 tram. The construction works in the city centre created huge problems for traffic, and shopkeepers suffered a dramatic reduction in customers; Lothian Buses saw a substantial fall in passenger numbers and a serious impact on its revenue.

## The competition

A few months after the decision to drop the CERT guided-busway scheme in 2001, First Edinburgh launched a competitive challenge to Lothian in Edinburgh with a network of high-frequency routes, including two that directly duplicated Lothian's successful 22 and 23 services. First cut its single and day fares, and Lothian responded by extending further into East Lothian and Midlothian. Lothian also had to put major capital investment on hold and rounded up a fleet of elderly Mk 1 Leyland Nationals to compete with First. It was also forced to cut daytime, evening and Sunday frequencies on many routes to counteract the loss in revenue following First's actions. But as so often happens the competition fizzled out within a year, First's losses prompting it to confine its operations to its traditional areas.

## The legacy

Ten years of Neil Renilson left Lothian in a very strong position, despite the recent problems caused by tram works. Lothian Buses management have been involved in the tram project for some time, and the bus and tram companies are moving closer together.

Neil left Lothian with a greatly modernised fleet, a better day and night route network, simpler fares, modernised garages, a more manageable central workshop, investment in technology like smartcards, kerbside ticket machines, real-time bus stop information and a GPS vehicle-location system. And it was a bus company that regularly won top awards — in fact one of the top bus companies in the UK. Not bad for 10 years' work.

**The Volvo B7RLE with Wright Eclipse bodywork became Lothian's standard single-deck purchase between 2004 and 2009. For the 1.5km Edinburgh Fastlink busway Lothian bought guidewheel-fitted B7RLEs. The busway is now being converted to become part of Edinburgh's new tramway.**

# Lancs Lynx let loose

**David Wayman** looks back to the day the National Bus Company's only Leyland Lynx entered service.

*All photographs by the author.*

Having calculated the bingo winnings that they would have had if only ... "Eeh, wot a posh new bus!" they exclaimed when I positioned the Leyland Lynx before them in the Boulevard bus station in Blackburn on that fine Sunday evening, 13 July 1986, just three months before deregulation. The vehicle certainly differed from their usual double-deck Bristol VRT or Leyland Olympian.

"Yes," responded their chauffeur. He might have added (but didn't): "And welcome aboard an example of the vehicle type that is meant to be the successor to the Leyland National. Although it's painted in a modified Ribble livery, this fine specimen still belongs to Leyland Bus, and we're trying it out."

The Lynx rear-engined single-deck bus as introduced in 1986 never would become prolific like the National. There was only ever that one example of the species, type LX1126LXCTFR1, in the fleet of Preston-based Ribble Motor Services, in those days a National Bus Company concern for which I drove part-time.

The Lynx, fleet number 901, was on its first revenue-earning journey, the 22.05 on service 233 to Grindleton, 14 miles north-easterly, up in the dramatic hills of the East Lancashire/West Yorkshire borderlands. Of course, on this journey the Lynx would hardly be over-worked, with relatively quiet roads and seldom more than a dozen folk aboard. The travellers remarked on the dual-height entrance step and lower first interior step, the ramped floor without the usual step just forward of the rear axle, and the moquette-covered seats. There were longitudinal seats over the front wheel arches, and immediately aft of these were a pair of double transverse rearward-facing seats on which no-one sat that Sunday.

Internally, with its black window surrounds the Lynx looked less like a dispensary than did the Leyland National. Nor had the Lynx the sophisticated heating and ventilating system of the National. The under-seat heaters were highly effective, however, which led to a little window-steaming.

Away we went northerly on highway A666, called Whalley New Road in that part of Blackburn. Soon we had covered the 2.5 miles from start to Brownhills junction and

**Ribble's new Leyland Lynx, out of service, visits Blackburn's Boulevard bus station earlier on the day of the journey described in the text. The Cumbria registration reveals it had been registered by Leyland's Workington factory, where it was built.**

**The Lynx ready to leave the depot to take up its first service journey as described. Although in Ribble colours it remained in Leyland ownership.**

turning right there, still on the A666, wove sedately eastwards through upmarket Wilpshire (3.0 miles, 11 minutes from start) and then on to Langho (5.2 miles, 18 minutes). Yes, the bus was indeed a single-deck Lynx and not a highbridge double-decker, on which the railway overbridge just ahead would have performed a hurried and noisy conversion.

Ribble's new big cat rode smoothly over indifferent road surfaces. Unlike Leyland Nationals of the Mk 1 variety in some circumstances, it showed no tendency to wallow or to roll on corners such as those at the sizeable roundabout by the Petre Arms, at the junction of the A666 and A59 roads. Here the manœuvre comprised a left-right weave followed by a wide right-hand sweep through 180° and then a moderate right tack so as to position for a sharp left flourish through about 120°. The Lynx behaved impeccably and made no attempt to emulate its Leyland National and National 2 predecessors, which at that location required severe slowing.

The four-speed fully automatic Hydracyclic gearbox was commendably smooth in operation, with snatch-free ratio changes, up and down. Take-off from rest was smart but not so sudden as to cause passengers to break into an involuntary sprint rearward after paying their fares. Of all the fully-auto models that I ever drove, including examples of the Leyland Olympian, National 2, and Dennis Javelin, only the solitary Bristol VRT that had a Maxwell 'box, Ribble's 2029, could compare with the Lynx for smoothness whether accelerating or decelerating.

With the Lynx, under normal conditions changes of ratio took effect as follows:

**Up** 1st to 2nd — 13mph
2nd to 3rd — 22mph
3rd to 4th — 34mph

**Down** 4th to 3rd — 25mph
3rd to 2nd — 16mph
2nd to 1st — 8mph

For an earlier change-down the 'hold' facility caused those speeds to be raised by about 15%. This proved useful when traffic conditions necessitated a drop in speed followed by acceleration. A quick flick of the lever into 'hold' at the same time as a further depressing of the accelerator pedal induced a rapid pick-up of speed. The Lynx's gearbox didn't appear to have a kick-down facility, or if it had, it wasn't working on this occasion, so that a one-ratio downward change couldn't be induced by a sharp pressing down of the accelerator pedal the full length of its travel.

Easterly now headed the cat over the gentle undulations of the A59 and down into Whalley (7.5 miles, 27 minutes), the village being in the shadow of the distinctive Whalley Nab (promontory) and also on the route of Ribble's service 723 (previously X23) linking Clitheroe with Manchester. The Lynx would share that route, more northerly now, creeping through tiny Barrow (9.5 miles), not to be confused with the considerably larger one 'in-Furness' 80 miles north and on the coast.

Turning left at the T junction, the Lynx padded moderately down into Clitheroe (10.7 miles, 41 minutes), site of another Ribble depot as well as the remains of a 12th-century castle. A small exchange of passengers took place at the town-centre stop in York Street before the new bus moved off and turned into and out of Well Terrace, near the Ribble depot, and then continued on a straight north-easterly course, hardly undulating and most easily timed. Two miles on there was a short, sharp descent to the picturesque village of Chatburn (12.9 miles, 51 minutes).

From Blackburn to this point the route of service 232 was the same as that of service 233, but in Chatburn the 232 branched right to climb sharply and continued for nearly a mile to pretty little Downham, high on touring organisations' lists of England's most attractive villages and in the shadow of the celebrated Pendle Hill, visible from many miles away and famed for its witches of earlier centuries. Up at Downham, for years buses had had to be reversed from a narrow road into their terminal point in a tight corner formed by buildings and without a footpath behind. Subsequently it was changed to a more amenable road junction.

Back down in Chatburn, however, Grindleton-bound buses on service 233 turned left and dropped down to the river named on their sides, zig-zagging over it on a narrow bridge. The short flat stretch on the other side led to a junction where a stop was necessary before a right-turn on to an ascent of 200 or 300 yards at 1-in-7 into Grindleton village. At full power, the Lynx took it admirably, even managing a change-up from 2nd to 3rd as it reached the top. Only the 'Maxwell' Bristol VRT could come anywhere near the Lynx's performance at that spot.

About 200 yards or more beyond the steep climb and in a housing area, about a bus-length or so past a short cul-de-sac on the left, buses stopped, and any remaining passengers alighted before reversal of the bus to the boarding point in the dead-end. The manœuvre was usually made more hazardous by the presence of cars parked at the alighting point and also in the rear of the bus's standing place at the boarding point. Subsequently the terminus was moved a few hundred yards to a much more suitable turning place.

All in all, a pleasant – and only slightly challenging – trip on which to break in Ribble's first (and last) Lynx.

***Above: En route* to Grindleton, and more typical of buses on the 233, an ECW-bodied Bristol VRT of 1977 turns into Clitheroe's York Street in October 1985.**

***Right:* The Grindleton terminus was moved in 1984 to this quiet spot, where an Olympian has attracted the attention of the local wildlife.**

***Above:*** **Ribble bus by River Ribble, just leaving Grindleton. The bus is one of 40 Leyland Nationals delivered to the company in 1973/4. It was photographed in April 1986.**

***Below:*** **Downham in April 1986, with a 1978 National ready to head back to Blackburn.**

# One, two, many

**October 1986 witnessed the deregulation of local bus services in Britain. David Cole considers its impact on the bus operations of a Midlands town.**

*All photographs by the author.*

The year 2011 marks the 25th anniversary of the deregulation of Britain's bus services outside London. It may not have delivered the aspirations of its original champions, who envisaged large numbers of small operators competing against each other, but the entrepreneurial approach has brought results. Subsidies have been reduced, and the process has been the catalyst to bringing some of the most cost-effective and highest-quality services in Europe to parts of Britain.

These successes are mainly associated with commercially viable networks in urban areas, where operators and local authorities have recognised the need to work in partnership to increase public transport's share of the travel market. There have, however, been major challenges in the shire counties, where many services rely on local-authority funding. Here passengers have had to accustom themselves to regular changes in timetables and operators, as local-authority budgets shrink and the big groups strive for profit margins that satisfy their investors.

This review focuses on a medium-sized town in a shire county. It is not intended to be a definitive record of all the changes which have taken place over the past quarter-century — more a review of significant events and vehicle policies which have influenced the perception of buses in the area.

The North Worcestershire town of Bromsgrove lies about 15 miles southwest of Birmingham and is the administrative centre of Bromsgrove District. Just over half the district's 80,000 residents live in the town; most of the others are in communities contiguous with the boundaries of the Birmingham and Black Country conurbation and have alternative focal points for shopping and entertainment. Despite significant reductions in the car-manufacturing industry which once dominated employment in the area, in 2008 Bromsgrove District had the highest percentage of its population in work of any authority outside London. The district is relatively affluent, and use of the bus as the mode of travel of choice is limited.

Bromsgrove has experienced most of deregulation's highs and lows – new and innovative services, seemingly pointless competition and service reductions, alongside quality and frequency improvements on the main corridor linking the town to Birmingham. From what was once almost a National Bus Company monopoly, through early deregulation which brought in another major player, the number of operators serving the town is now close to double figures, many more having come and gone in the intervening years.

It could have been very different. Back in 1969 Bromsgrove was within the original boundaries of the West Midlands Passenger Transport Authority, but in 1974, when local government was reorganised, the expanded Bromsgrove District was placed in the new county of Hereford & Worcester and was thus excluded from PTA influence. Bus services remained under the

**Devoid of fleetnames pending the creation of West Midlands Travel, a WMPTE Leyland Lynx arrives in Bromsgrove on one of the first post-deregulation journeys on service 145 from Birmingham in late August 1986.**

**Red Arrow Express, trading as Little Red Bus, operated several Worcestershire tendered services in the 1990s. This Northern Counties-bodied Dodge minibus was new to GM Buses and still displays its original owner's 'I'm a Little Gem' legend above the windscreen.**

control of NBC's Midland Red, increasingly subsidised by the County Council, and relatively little progress would be made in developing local rail services from the town's rather remote station.

Despite some retrenchment, Bromsgrove's Midland Red network of 1974 was broadly that which had been established during the company's early development. The core was the 144 Birmingham–Malvern Wells trunk route, supported by regular-interval interurban services to Redditch, Stourbridge and Halesowen, a few rural links and two 'back roads' routes from Birmingham, one of which ran on a limited-stop basis and continued to Worcester, Gloucester or Cheltenham. Most town services were provided by extensions or diversions of the inter-urban services.

A significant shake-up of services occurred in 1979 when Midland Red's MAP (Market Analysis Project) reached the area, Bromsgrove being included in Worcester's new Severnlink network. The principal change was the curtailment of the 144 at Worcester on a reduced frequency and the introduction of an alternative 143 to give four direct departures an hour from Birmingham. The 143 followed an alternative route into Bromsgrove, covering the urban part of the much-reduced Halesowen service and a link to Redditch. The limited-stop service to Birmingham ceased, the element over the Lickey Hills being incorporated into a new Halesowen service routed through expanding residential areas on the Birmingham/ Bromsgrove boundary. Most services were by then operated by Leyland Nationals or dual-purpose Leyland Leopards.

It was the MAP network that formed the basis of the deregulation service registrations although Midland Red West, Midland Red's successor in the area, determined that, in addition to many evening and Sunday services, the Halesowen and Birmingham (via Barnt Green) services were not commercially viable. These were put out to tender by Hereford & Worcester County, the successful bidder for many being the soon-to-be 'arm's-length' WMPTE operation, West Midlands Travel. Deregulation came early to Bromsgrove, the new service pattern being implemented at the end of August 1986, two months before 'D-Day' itself. West Midlands Travel was out to impress, and the tendered services were operated by the company's early-production batch of Leyland Lynxes, less than a year old and freshly repainted in standard livery. Their sojourn was short, however, and soon Leyland Nationals were the norm.

Although a local minibus operator initially registered a number of town services, these did not materialise, and early-deregulation Bromsgrove was basically a two-operator town. The now privatised Midland Red West regained some of its losses the following year, starting the unending pattern of route and operator changes, which are best considered on a route or route-group basis.

## Birmingham direct

The 143/144 combination established at MAP proved the most enduring aspect of the operations of Midland Red West and its successor, First, through Bromsgrove, experiencing only minor changes for nearly 20 years. In the mid-1990s the commercial Sunday service was reduced to a two-hourly frequency, prompting the County Council to award a contract to Birmingham-based Little Red Bus/Red Arrow Express to retain an hourly frequency. As the name implies, the company provided red-painted (Dodge) minibuses, which at times proved inadequate for the traffic on offer. Midland Red West retained Leyland Nationals on the 144 until 1995, when appropriate MRW-registered Plaxton Verde-bodied Dennis Lances from Worcester garage took over. The 143 gained Leyland Lynxes from Redditch garage where the company's batch of 50 had all congregated.

*Right:* **Go-Ahead's Diamond Bus started running to Bromsgrove in June 2005. The first-ever departure was worked by an ex-Metrobus Optare Excel, seen heading northwards along Market Street.**

*Below:* **Congestion in the bus station led to the creation of a layover bay behind Asda. In April 2009 a Red Diamond Volvo B7RLE/Wright was resting between journeys on the 64 although already branded for the company's competitive foray on the 144 route, which was about to commence.**

All changed in July 2005. First diverted the 144 to cover most of the 143's approach to the town, the Birmingham section of the 143 being withdrawn. The remainder of the 143 to Redditch was halved in frequency, just a few journeys being extended to the northern suburbs of Bromsgrove. Halving the Birmingham–Bromsgrove frequency opened up an opportunity for Diamond Bus, then owned by Go-Ahead, to extend its 64 service from the Birmingham boundary into Bromsgrove half-hourly via the original 144 route. First reacted quickly and increased the frequency of the 144 to three buses an hour. All changed again in April 2009 when Diamond Bus, by now part of Rotala and branded as Red Diamond, withdrew its 64 service between Birmingham and Bromsgrove and replaced it with a half-hourly Birmingham–Bromsgrove 144 service in direct competition with First. The through service to Birmingham did not last long, being curtailed early in 2010 as a 144E at the Rubery Great Park shopping and entertainment complex, although the frequency was increased to three buses an hour.

When first its route was extended to Bromsgrove, Diamond Bus used Optare Excels on the 64, these later being superseded by various Dennis Lances and Darts. For the 144, route-branded one-year-old Wright Eclipse-bodied Volvo B7RLEs were introduced by Red Diamond, although the route reverted to Darts following curtailment at Rubery. Wright Eclipse Volvos were also transferred within First to Worcester, supplanting the Alexander Dennis Enviro300s introduced in 2005 and running alongside most of the small batch of Alexander ALX400-bodied Dennis Tridents which had brought regular public double-deck operation back to Bromsgrove for the first time in nearly 20 years.

First's 143 also underwent major changes in 2009, restoring an hourly connection to Birmingham via the

**Double-deckers returned to First's operations in Bromsgrove on the 144 in 2008. Normally these were Alexander ALX400-bodied Tridents, but occasionally older vehicles made an appearance. This Alexander-bodied Olympian, seen in February 2009, was originally in the Grampian fleet and has undergone a rather crude conversion from dual-door layout.**

original 144 route and taking on an additional role of a town service to the south-east of Bromsgrove, covering some previously unserved roads and restoring First services to the Charford estate.

## Town services

At deregulation the incorporation of town services into inter-urban routes had left the link to the Charford estate as the only one with a regular local service. Not surprisingly, given Midland Red West's leading role in introducing high-frequency minibus networks, this was soon rejuvenated with minibuses using the 'Shuttle' branding launched initially in Kidderminster. There followed a frequent minibus service to Catshill, north of the town centre – a facility First was to incorporate into the diverted 144 in 2005.

The Charford service was to experience direct competition from Rover Coaches and later Clearway Taxis, First withdrawing what had become an isolated operation in 2006. The increased Clearway service used Plaxton Beaver 2-bodied Mercedes-Benz Varios. First returned to Charford in 2009 with the diverted 143.

Long-established local coach operator Rover Coaches had changed ownership in 1988 following the retirement of its proprietor, Mrs Brown. The new owner, Dave Stephenson, rapidly implemented a comprehensive network of local routes throughout Bromsgrove under the title 'The Bromsgrove Rover', using unusual Lex-bodied

**Carlyle minibus competition in Bromsgrove during November 1990. The Rover Ford Transit still carries 'Skipper' branding from its days with East Yorkshire, a company which had family connections with Rover at the time. Redline's first minibus, a Freight Rover Sherpa, originated with Busways in Newcastle.**

**MRD Travel brought the Stagecoach colour scheme to Bromsgrove with three Alexander Sprint-bodied Mercedes minibuses. With the bus station trees in full blossom in April 2006, the first example, which originated with Midland Red South, departs on the twice-weekly service to Dodford, a village west of Bromsgrove.**

Leyland Cubs previously with R&I in North London. These linked the town centre and railway station with the mainly private housing estates which had developed around the town in the previous 20 years. The services were probably ahead of their time for the then car-fixated population, and most were short-lived. Parts of the network did, however, provide useful links, and when Rover planned their withdrawal the County Council put them up for tender. Perhaps to its surprise, Rover failed to regain them in the tender award and then ran for a period in competition with the winning bidder, Redline, bringing the town's first instance of seemingly pointless competition. It did, however, provide the opportunity for a direct comparison of the relative merits of the original Carlyle minibus body on Ford Transit and Freight Rover Sherpa chassis. Rover eventually withdrew.

Redline was a product of deregulation, established by former Midland Red West staff to operate competitively using double-deckers in Redditch. This operation ended abruptly, and Redline re-emerged under the proprietorship of Stan Pemberton, winning a package of contracted work, including the routes which were operated for a time in competition with Rover. Starting with one Freight Rover minibus, the Redline fleet grew to five immaculately maintained vehicles on a network including alternative commercial routes to Catshill and Charford. Flagships were two unusual ECB-bodied Ivecos bought new, and the company was planning to order larger midibuses when it all ended abruptly (again!) in 1997. Citing the difficulty of recruiting and retaining suitable staff, it ceased trading overnight. Midland Red West stepped in to provide temporary cover, pending re-tendering, on routes where the companies had not been in competition.

Further re-tendering in the new millennium brought in Pete's Travel and then Cofton Hire, a South Birmingham operator new to local services in Bromsgrove. The latter company now provides a single Mercedes-Benz minibus to coach specification.

MRD Travel, a new operation started by Mark Davies, commenced a commercial town service to parts of Catshill not otherwise served in 2004, dovetailing with a recently awarded council contract for a twice-weekly circular to villages west of Bromsgrove. The service was a success, due not least to the high level of customer service offered, and soon outgrew the LDV 400 minibus in use. Replacement came in the form of an ex-Stagecoach Alexander Sprint-bodied Mercedes-Benz minibus, with a second in reserve. Journeys to Charford have subsequently been added to the morning-only operation.

## The Halesowen services

By deregulation the original link from Bromsgrove to Halesowen via Romsley had become a shadow of its former self, with just a small number of supported journeys. Regular operation on the route was re-established in 1994 when Halesowen-based Ludlows Coaches extended its 007 Merry Hill–Romsley service through to Bromsgrove and then non-stop to Redditch shopping centre and district hospital, providing, in particular, new facilities for shoppers. Starting with Volvo-repowered Leyland Nationals and early Carlyle-bodied Darts, the route was one of the first in the area to be operated with low-floor buses – Wright-bodied Dennis Darts. The Redditch extension was relatively short-lived, but the core route was to survive to 2009, by which time Ludlows had been acquired by Rotala and incorporated into the Diamond Bus operation.

The replacement County Council-supported service brought to Bromsgrove another new operator, Midland Rider, with one bus providing a link on a 90-minute frequency to Halesowen only. The new service incorporated a diversion in Romsley to serve a park home development which had gained its first bus connection earlier in the year, a shuttle service connecting with the 007 operated by MRD Travel. In early 2010 some journeys on the 007 were extended across Bromsgrove to serve the large new housing development at the Oakhalls.

In comparison, the alternative 202 service to Halesowen, established in the 1980s, has seen little change in route or frequency, although the operator changed regularly in the early days of deregulation. Following a brief return to Midland Red West, it was taken up in 1989 by Stevensons of Uttoxeter, which continued to operate it until withdrawing from the West Midlands in 1994. Several of the Stevensons vehicles wore blue fronts with the original WMPTE logo – a glimpse of what might have been, had the political changes of 1974 been different. The route then passed to Ludlows on a mainly commercial basis, being progressively upgraded from step-entrance Carlyle-bodied Darts to two generations of Wright-bodied low-floor Scanias. With Ludlows incorporation into Rotala's Diamond Bus the 202 became the only Diamond Bus route into Bromsgrove to be operated under the Black Diamond branding used for Black Country routes.

Soon after Ludlows had become established on both Halesowen routes, the autumn of 1996 brought the second round of pointless competition to Bromsgrove. Rivalry between Ludlows and the Birmingham Coach Company in the Black Country spilled over into the town, the latter registering competing journeys on both Halesowen services, initially running free and often running duplicates to reinforce the message. Both companies relied mainly on old Leyland Nationals, and Bromsgrove bus station was unhealthily crowded with them at times. Having failed to break Ludlows' resolve, the Birmingham Coach Company withdrew, but its apparent aims were achieved some 15 years later, when both companies found themselves in Rotala ownership.

## Birmingham via Barnt Green

The only route out of Bromsgrove with restricted headroom caused by a low bridge, the 145, linked communities on the eastern slopes of the Lickey Hills, although the largest of these, Barnt Green, benefited from a regular rail service on Birmingham's cross-city line. Following the changes at deregulation the route became a Tame Valley operation using a mixture of Leyland Nationals and minibuses. In 1991 it passed to Birmingham-based Careline, with one-time West Midlands Travel Sherpa minibuses. This proved to be short-lived, as did Stevensons' subsequent tenure, and from the end of 1991 there ensued a long period of operation by West Midlands Travel from Yardley Wood depot, reintroducing the Leyland Lynx.

When Travel West Midlands started shedding marginal routes outside its core area the 145 was one of the last to go, in July 2003, taking with it the hourly frequency and the through journeys to Birmingham. The County-supported successor terminated at King's Norton station in Birmingham's southern suburbs, and a 90-minute frequency could be achieved with the one vehicle supplied

**In October 1996 competition broke out between Ludlows and the Birmingham Coach Company, the latter running free services for a time. Here Ludlows' former PMT Leyland National, already more than 20 years old, passes a slightly younger example from the Birmingham Coach Company fleet on the commercial 007 service from Redditch to Merry Hill.**

***Right:*** **The last Travel West Midlands journey on the 145 arrives in Bromsgrove in July 2003, complete with 'Last 145' bill in the nearside windscreen. The refurbished Leyland Lynx was one of a small number to gain TWM's 'low-floor' livery.**

***Below:*** **In April 2006 a Zak's Mini Pointer Dart awaits departure from Bromsgrove bus station on the truncated 145 service via the low bridge in Barnt Green to Cotteridge station. Behind it are a Ludlows Scania (on the 202) and a First Dennis Lance.**

by Zak's Travel. Zak's was one of Rotala's first acquisitions and initially brought the Central Connect brand to the service, later replaced by Red Diamond upon transfer to Diamond Buses' growing Worcestershire operation.

## Stourbridge

With the exception of additional peak-hour and Sunday supported services, Midland Red West/First continued the 318 Stourbridge service on an hourly frequency into the new millennium. Replacement by Hansons of Stourbridge saw the normal daytime departures move to 100-minute intervals to facilitate one-vehicle operation and introduce a double run in Bromsgrove to provide an additional link to the town's community hospital.

## The Hospital Link

One of the more innovative new services introduced since deregulation was driven by changes to NHS provision in North Worcestershire. Bromsgrove and Redditch had shared a district hospital on the eastern outskirts of Redditch since the mid-1980s, meaning at least one and often two changes of bus were needed for Bromsgrove residents. In addition the NHS withdrew many services from Kidderminster hospital in favour of facilities in Redditch and Worcester. To ease the changes, new bus services with NHS and County support were introduced in 2000, Bromsgrove being the mid-point of the X33 linking Kidderminster and Redditch hospitals. First was successful in the tender process and transferred some Plaxton Beaver-

*Above:* **At the peak of operations in Worcestershire during 2002 Pete's Travel ran both the X33 and 98 services in Bromsgrove. The 98 was normally minibus-operated, but occasionally Darts were used. The bus on the left was acquired new for the X33 and wears the orange front applied to vehicles operated on Worcestershire services.**

*Below:* **The route-branded Dart/Pointers supplied by First for the X33 hospital connection were removed when NHS support for the service was withdrawn. In the summer of 2005 Bromsgrove's bus terminus was temporarily relocated to the rear of the Asda store.**

**Clearway's operation of the 78 service to Redditch via Blakenhurst prison in the mid-1990s used a variety of lift-equipped former local-authority vehicles. This Bedford VAS5 had utilitarian-looking bodywork by Dormobile.**

bodied Mercedes-Benz Varios from Bradford Traveller to Kidderminster for its operation, tight timings meaning an hourly frequency could just be achieved with two vehicles. One duty was soon handed over to the only low-floor bus then in First Midland Red's fleet, a Pointer-bodied Dart.

Re-tendering in 2002 brought a new operator in the form of Pete's Travel, the growing Black Country company with a recently established Worcestershire base in the former Midland Red depot at Redditch. New low-floor Darts with an orange Worcestershire front on their yellow Plaxton Pointer bodies were introduced, but service quality declined rapidly. In 2003 the County pulled the plug on Pete's Travel's tendered operations, and First took back the X33, using assorted mainly low-floor vehicles, now in Barbie livery. However, Pete's Travel refused to give up, so, for a third time, Bromsgrove saw pointless competition as the company attempted to maintain its presence on the service with an assortment of mainly step-entrance Darts.

During 2004 First invested significantly in the X33, introducing new route-branded Pointer Darts. Three were now required for the service, which had been diverted to include Bromsgrove Community Hospital. Less than two years later NHS funding was withdrawn, and First reconfigured the core service as a link from the western suburbs of Kidderminster to Redditch bus station, eliminating the hospital links and substituting mainly step-entrance Dennis Lances for the Darts. Services outside the core were put out to tender, some journeys being retained by First and others passing to Johnson's of Henley. Most of the latter were short-lived due to loss of patronage but brought significant vehicle variety to the town as Johnson's tried out a number of demonstrators as well as the first of its Optare Tempos.

## Other services

The communities to the east of the 144 route between Bromsgrove and Droitwich are linked to Bromsgrove by the 140/141 service, operated by Red Diamond on an hourly basis from 2009. Prior to this, other than for a brief Little Red Bus interlude in the mid-1990s, the service had been operated by Midland Red West/First, latterly on a partial 'Roamer Bus' (pre-booking) basis using some of the last First minibuses to operate in the area.

In the 1990s a direct service was provided for visitors to the prisons between Bromsgrove and Redditch. Initially this was operated by Clearway with various lift-equipped minibuses, later passing to First.

Alongside schools work, contracted mainly to local coach operators, a registered school bus service was introduced by the Green Bus Company in 2006. This links Kidderminster with King Edward's School in Birmingham via a circuitous route through Bromsgrove and is operated with double-deckers. In-house provision of vehicles followed an initial year of contracted operation by First in full Green Bus colours.

Prior to the introduction of the X33 Bromsgrove had been linked to Kidderminster by a variety of irregular services, one of which, the 197, was operated for a period by Go Whittle. Another irregular service has for several years linked Bromsgrove with Redditch via communities on the southern slopes of the Lickey Hills.

## Short-lived innovations

In the early 1990s certain journeys on the County-supported 177/178 Birmingham–Wythall–Redditch service, then operated by Rover Coaches, were extended to Bromsgrove. These provided the first direct link with the town for Bromsgrove District residents in the Wythall

**The only regular double-deck operation into Bromsgrove during the first 20 years of deregulation was provided by Rover Coaches on Saturday journeys on service 177. The vehicle used was a former Keighley & District Bristol VRT, seen heading south along Market Street in the autumn of 1994. The only other instance of double-deck operation in the town at that time involved the occasional appearance of a West Midlands Travel Fleetline on the 202.**

area, most of whom associated themselves with Birmingham or Solihull. An attraction was the use of a Bristol VRT double-decker on Saturday departures, the first regular double-decker operation in Bromsgrove for many years. The bus came from Keighley & District, by now a fellow Blazefield company following the group's acquisition of Rover. In 1996 Rover was absorbed into the Cambridge Coach Services operation, remaining as an outstation for that company's Midlands–Cambridge service until its withdrawal.

As part of its franchise commitments for the West Coast main line, Virgin Trains introduced a number of express coach links to its railheads. In 1999 Bromsgrove was linked via Redditch to Birmingham International station, potentially a very attractive idea given the latter's proximity to Birmingham airport. Smart modern Berkhof-bodied Volvo coaches in Virgin colours were provided by Stagecoach Warwickshire (better known as Midland Red South), but patronage was disappointing, and the service ceased. Stagecoach Warwickshire had also provided the vehicles for Bromsgrove's last remaining National Express coach service, a daily Kidderminster–London journey. The cessation of this brought to an end the town's long coaching tradition, which had encompassed coaching inns and most Associated Motorways services to/from the South West.

## A retrospective

Even this short overview clearly shows that change has been a constant of the period since deregulation and that, if anything, the pace of change is accelerating. Often this is not good news for marginal passengers – those for whom use of the bus is a matter of choice above other transport modes. Stability is important to them, even if the concept is not popular with the Competition Commission. Knowing that there will be a bus to take them to work, college or wherever for the foreseeable future can be an important element in their choice of employment or education, cost being relative to other modes. In parallel, county councils do a good job in using their restricted funding to ensure service provision for those without other transport options.

Bromsgrove's experiences have been replicated in many towns across Britain, and recalling them serves as a reminder that for transport enthusiasts deregulation created much of interest in terms both of operations and of the vehicles used thereon.

**The short-lived connecting service to Birmingham International station was operated for Virgin Trains by Stagecoach Midland Red using colourful Berkhof-bodied Volvo B10Ms. Loadings were poor, as evidenced by this example northbound in Market Street in May 2000.**

# Berkhof bonanza

**Not all National Bus Company coaches were bodied by Duple and Plaxton. Geoff Mills looks back at the Berkhof interlude at London Country.**

In 1982 Ensignbus of Purfleet, Essex, was appointed UK distributor for Berkhof bodywork, built in Valkenswaard, Holland. A demonstrator based on a Volvo B10M chassis was duly imported and in August 1982 was sold to Harwich & Dovercourt Coaches.

A more significant demonstrator, new in September 1983, was in 1984 repainted for NBC's London Country Bus Services fleet, in Green Line livery. It was a high-floor Everest based on a DAF MB200 chassis and worked from Dunton Green depot in Kent, but did not receive a fleet number. Coincidentally, a Berkhof-bodied DAF, but a standard-height Esprite, was supplied to London Transport around the same time.

The demonstrator at London Country clearly made a good impression, and the company quickly placed large orders with Ensignbus. These formed a new BTL class (Berkhof Tiger Lengthened), and 25 were supplied between October 1984 and January 1985, followed by a further eight in the summer of 1985 and a final 20 in the first five months of 1986. All were based on the 12m Tiger TRCTL11/3RH chassis, with Hydracyclic gearbox, and had Everest 370 bodies, a few with bus-type entrance doors. There was a variety of interior specifications, as well as a range of liveries including Green Line, Flightline, Insight International, Jetlink, National Express, National Holidays and Town & Country.

In September 1986 London Country was split into four regional companies — South East, South West, North East and North West. The bulk of the BTLs — 38 — went to London Country South West, smaller numbers going to LCSE (11) and LCNW (4). In later life most found further use with

***Below:*** **The original Green Line demonstrator was a DAF MB200 with 49-seat Esprite 370 body, the figure indicating the vehicle's height in centimetres. Delivered to Ensignbus in a white-based livery in the autumn of 1983, it was in the spring of 1984 repainted in the standard Green Line livery of the time, two-tone green with a white roof. It carried London Country legal lettering but was not allocated a fleet number. It had a deeper and more upright windscreen than the Tigers which followed.**

small coach operators, but in 1991 eight were purchased by Midland Red North – a sister company of London Country South West within the Drawlane group — and fitted with new 61-seat East Lancs EL2000 bus bodies.

As a state-owned business, NBC sourced the vast majority of its new vehicles from British manufacturers and London Country's 53 Berkhof bodies marked its biggest single investment in full-size European-built vehicles.

***Above:*** **This Tiger, seen in 1992 in the ownership of County Bus (itself formed from London Country North East), shows the bus-style doors specified on a minority of the Berkhof bodies. When new this coach was in Jetlink livery.**

***Below:*** **There were eight Jetlink-liveried coaches in the initial batch of 25 BTLs, and these were two-tone green with cream relief on the lower panels and roof. They were 53-seaters and were for operation on airport services to Heathrow and Gatwick. This one is heading to Heathrow from Luton in 1990; by this time it was part of the LCSW fleet.**

***Left:*** **A small number of BTLs wore National Express livery – some from new, others, including this coach, later in their lives. This LCSW coach is seen in Brighton in 1992 and would be sold the following year.**

***Below left:*** **In London's Victoria Coach Station in December 1984 a new BTL waits to take up service on the Flightline 777 service to Gatwick. It was a 53-seater with bus-style doors. The dot-matrix destination display fitted to most BTLs is just visible above the horizontal bar which splits the windscreen in two. When new the main lower section of the windscreen was a single piece of glass; later in life many BTLs acquired split screens.**

***Below:*** **The last five of the original batch of BTLs were 53-seaters delivered in tour-company liveries – three for Town & Country and two for Insight International. This one is seen in Crawley, participating in the 1985 British Coach Rally and carries Leyland's Tiger badge. The only clue that this is a London Country coach is the fleet number, applied ahead of the front wheel.**

***Above:*** **The eight coaches delivered in the summer of 1985 were for the new Speedlink service between Heathrow and Gatwick airports, using a newly opened section of the M25 motorway. They were 37-seaters, offering airline passengers a high standard of comfort. The seats were grouped around tables. This one is seen a bit off route, in Luton in 1990. By this time it was owned by Speedlink Airport Services, which had been created in 1989 as a separate company within the Drawlane group, owner of LCSW since 1988.**

***Above right:*** **The 20 coaches delivered in 1986 were generally similar to the two previous batches. All were 53-seaters, although this vehicle, seen at that year's British Coach Rally, has been temporarily down-seated and fitted with tables.**

***Right:*** **Five of the 1986 coaches started life in National Holidays livery. A 1987 view at Scratchwood Services on the M1 motorway shows holidaymakers heading off for the Peak District and Chester.**

***Left:*** **The last five of London Country's Berkhof Tigers initially carried Insight International livery. Three of these were among the 11 coaches which were inherited by London Country South East. By 1992 this example was in Kentish Express colours, and despite being six years old was participating in the UK Coach Rally. LCSE had been renamed the Kentish Bus & Coach Co in 1987 and was privatised the following year when it was bought by Proudmutual.**

***Above:*** **The Kentish fleetname above the front wheel reveals the ownership of this Tiger, seen in 1990 on contract to Shearings National.**

***Left:*** **The Countryliner name was adopted by LCSW in 1992 for its coach-hire business. Although 10 years old when photographed at Chessington in 1996 this Tiger still looks very smart. Countryliner still exists, now as an independent company.**

*Top:* **While London & Country bought 53 Berkhofs in the mid-1980s, London Transport also tried a Berkhof-bodied coach, running this DAF MB200 with 53-seat Esprite body. It entered service in 1984 with fleet number TC1 – TC for Tours & Charter.**

*Below left:* **The London & Country Berkhof-bodied Tigers proved popular with smaller operators when they became available on the second-hand market. This one joined the fleet of Kenmargra Coaches in West Yorkshire in 1993 and when photographed at Wembley the following year had acquired a home-made grille.**

## POSTSCRIPT

*Below:* **Eight LCSW BTLs found a new lease of life in the early 1990s, being rebodied as service buses for Midland Red North; both LCSW and Midland Red North were part of the Drawlane group. The new East Lancs bodies were 61-seaters. This view shows one in Tamworth in 1999.**
KEN JUBB

# One and only

**Tony Greaves has driven many interesting vehicles over the years. Here he selects a few based on the theme of one – number ones, firsts and only ones.**

*All photographs by the author.*

I have always considered myself to have an unusual working life. How does a trained artist end up driving all sorts of buses and coaches, ranging from the normal fare, through unusual vehicles to prototypes and downright oddballs? Back in the 1970s I had been working as a graphic designer (for which you needed then to be able to draw, as there were no computers), when my employer, along with many others in the Leeds area, closed down the studio in response to aggressive union activity and I, along with hundreds of others, was out of a job. My answer to this situation was to take a sabbatical from commercial art and apply to West Yorkshire PTE, successor to the sadly departed Leeds City Transport, for a position within that organisation. My intention was always that it would be only for a year or so, until the dust settled.

It turned out to be 15 months. I thoroughly enjoyed it, but didn't wish to waste my training, or, indeed, be still at a stop-gap job 30 years later, as many of my new colleagues were. I served as a conductor for three months, which automatically meant that it was time to enter the driving school, resulting in my being the proud possessor of a PSV driving licence, together with the accompanying badge. Upon my return to the world of graphic design I decided, now I had diesel in my blood, to keep my licence up and seek casual driving work. Thus began more than 26 years of the strange mix of artwork with driving for light relief.

### Wallace Arnold TUB 1M (my first '1')

Leyland Leopards (and a few AEC Reliances) with Plaxton Panorama Elite bodies were the standard at Wallace Arnold in the 1970s, the last Bedfords and Fords having recently being ousted from the fleet. Most of my driving jobs for 'Wally's' (Wallace Arnold to non-Yorkshiremen) in the first year or two were evening and weekend tour feeders. I must have gained approval from the right quarters, as that

**One of the days out on the author's Swiss trip involved a drop-off in Montreux, which presented the opportunity for this shot of his steed alongside an immaculate 20-year-old Saurer trolleybus of the Vevey-Montreux-Chillon-Villeneuve fleet. He particularly liked the alternating flashes on the higher and lower parts of its indicators when moving out.**

**GCN 1N, a North East bus now based in Yorkshire, pauses in Doncaster alongside a native Yorkshire Ailsa, in the shape of a South Yorkshire Transport bus with Van Hool McArdle body.**

changed in 1978 when I was asked if I would like to be part of a two-man team due to take a school party to Switzerland. As I have always loved Switzerland my answer was positive and delivered within milliseconds!

The day of departure arrived, and the other driver, a full-timer by the name of Geoff, and I were allocated our coach, a standard Leopard/Panorama Elite, with the memorable registration TUB 1M. After leaving the school we made for Dover with reasonable haste, as we had a ferry to catch. Once on French soil we kept driving, changing places every three hours or so, and eventually arrived at Leysin, high in the Alps, at around 2.30 in the morning. Leysin is about 6,000ft up, and reaching it involved more than half an hour of mountain-hairpin driving. The Leopard coped very well, but it was accepted that we stayed in 'crawler' and kept it going. Had we stopped it would have been very difficult to set off again.

We stayed at Leysin (made famous mere months previously by an Abba concert at the local ice rink) for a week. During that week we ferried the party to various places of interest, but the only notable incident happened on our day off. The teachers decided to take their charges on a mountain hike, mainly because it cost almost nothing at a time when the exchange rate was very unfavourable towards the pound. (Sound familiar?) Upon their return we were informed that several of the children had sun-stroke, others had frostbite through walking in snowdrifts and one unfortunate had both, the whole exercise costing the teachers' emergency fund dear!

### Independent Coachways GCN 1N (my second '1')

I had known the then owner of Independent Coachways of Horsforth, Tony Edwards, for several years through our shared interest in the Samuel Ledgard company, where he had worked in the traffic office. Indeed, he founded the Independent company using an ex-Ledgard Burlingham Seagull. Another ex-Ledgard employee, Barry Rennison, also worked for Independent, at first as a driver and eventually as Manager (from which post he is shortly to retire). They had both persuaded me to come along and 'do a bit'. So started a parallel life driving for Independent as well as 'Wally's' which continued for over a quarter of a century. I would hasten to add, of course, that I kept an eye on my hours.

One day Barry asked me if I knew of any decent double-deckers for sale. I drew his attention to the three pre-production Volvo Ailsas in storage at Tyne & Wear PTE and for sale as a result of industrial action. Apparently the drivers had blacked them because their automatic gearboxes had very fierce changes, no doubt aggravated by their free-revving engines. A couple of weeks later I was at Independent for another job and was pleasantly surprised that our conversation had produced results, for here were all three buses. A deal had been done which also included a quantity of spares. Preparation for Independent service included a repaint into the company's very attractive green, black and white livery and the fitting of semi-automatic control to the gearboxes, making them very pleasant buses to drive.

Perhaps because they wouldn't have been there but for our conversation, I was pleased to be the first driver to take one out. This was an evening job on a Friday, with GCN 2N. It, like the others, looked impressive in its new livery and, being only about five years old and having seen very little use, was very tidy inside. The following Sunday I was down to take a large party of scouts to an outdoor meeting in the Newcastle area! And it was No 1 that I had. What a bus. I could forgive its looks (I've never been a fan of Alexander's peaked domes) because it was such a delight to drive. My first cars were Citroën GSs with hydropneumatic suspension and brakes and I could feel a similar action when using the hydraulic brakes on these three pre-production Ailsas. All three enjoyed an eight-year stay at Independent, and I drove each of them on many occasions, including enthusiast-group trips. I took the opportunity of photographing GCN 1N alongside any local bus I saw, resulting in many unusual posed pairings.

### Independent Coachways PWY 31W (a 'one-off')

In the 1970s Independent Coachways had rebodied several Leyland Leopard chassis from a variety of sources, culminating in the appearance of ANW 21S. This was as far as the rebodying process could go, it was thought. But no. Apparently 31 was to have been an MAN SR280 integral coach, but the order was cancelled, and work started on the last of the 'Independent Leylands'.

When completed 31 might have been described as a visual mongrel, as the otherwise standard Plaxton Supreme IV body incorporated a deep Viewmaster windscreen, with a correspondingly shallow front panel, and tapered 'export' rear end. At first glance it might have been mistaken for a standard Leyland Leopard with a Supreme body, though the more inquisitive would soon pick up that this attractive coach was something quite different. Underneath, the mix was even more radical, with components coming from varied sources, including Tiger brakes and DAF fuel tanks. The *pièce d'resistance* was the engine, an overhauled O.600 Atlantean unit fitted in-line and turbocharged! As a reminder to all drivers and passengers that they were travelling in something a bit special, the Leyland Pneumocyclic gearchange pedestal unit was chrome-plated.

I drove 31 several times, the most memorable being a trip to Manchester Airport, and was impressed by the lack of engine noise. This could be thought of as a disadvantage, but with an eye on the rev counter clean gear changes were easy. The main criticism of 31 was that the front end was very light and the back end had a tendency to wander — hardly surprising, with the huge lump of Leyland engine at its hindmost extremity! In many ways 31 was a precursor of things to come in terms of its low noise levels, passenger appeal and comfort, features which were to become more widespread with the growth in sales of Continental rear-engined coaches.

**The rear cooling grille gives the clue that this one-off coach is no ordinary Leyland.**

### Ward C11-640 (the first unbodied chassis I had ever driven)

By 1983 I was self-employed and found myself assisting with the print and publicity needs of the Ward brothers, who were to launch a new coach chassis, the main benefits of which were to be simplicity, in the face of other manufacturers' increasing complexity, and ruggedness. Two brothers (the third remained as Manager of the Ward Bros coach company) had set up the new operation in Shepley, near Huddersfield.

**The author clearly enjoying himself with the Ward C11-640 chassis.**

We were to photograph the chassis, which was specially painted for display with the frame picked out in red and other components in various colours, for the product brochure, on one of the nearby lanes. I was offered a drive, so naturally I accepted. It was unlike any sensation I had ever experienced — the loud rasp of the Perkins V8 engine, the rapid acceleration and the feeling the wind in my face, all a result of the fact that it was an unbodied chassis.

On the official opening day of Ward Motors the display chassis took pride of place in the centre of the factory building, surrounded by flowers and flowing white fabric. Some of the photographs were used in the brochure, by which time the coach had been named the Ward Dalesman. Shortly afterwards the company went into receivership, and I had no further contact with the brothers. The chassis I had driven ultimately received a Plaxton Paramount body and joined the Abbeyways fleet in Halifax.

### Black Prince MGE 185P (emphatically a 'one-off')

I had got to know the Crowther family, owners of Black Prince, through production meetings for their holiday tours brochure. Once Brian Crowther realised I had a PSV licence he would often ask me to cover staff days off.

**Black Prince's single-deck Ailsa seen on its usual route, the 87, linking Holbeck with Pudsey.**

They were usually two-man coach jobs, but now and again it was local bus work, often with Ailsas or Routemasters, which I hadn't done for many years. Jack Berry, the Traffic Manager, was always keen to promote the company, so on many occasions a Black Prince bus attended rallies and picked up some silverware. I was asked if I fancied taking 185 to the 1994 Meadowhall Rally.

The bus had started life with Greater Glasgow PTE as a panoramic-windowed Alexander-bodied Volvo Ailsa, but in middle age it was found to have severe structural problems. It was beyond economic repair, so the same solution was applied as had been to some Atlanteans some years earlier: the top deck was removed. This was rather drastic and did nothing for the æsthetics of what had been a nice-looking bus! And, judging from pictures of it, the structural defects weren't cured.

The bus itself had gained the nickname 'The Slug', with more than a touch of irony. I soon discovered why when I drove it. Ailsas were always brisk in their progress, but without the weight of a top deck and staircase it was a veritable flying machine, and we were at Meadowhall in no time. 'The Slug', Jack and I appeared on the front cover of *Buses* later that year, but by the time the magazine was published the bus had gone. Apparently Strathclyde (as Greater Glasgow became) had failed to provide a document showing that the bus was now a single-decker! Brian and son David had decided that it wasn't worth spending several thousand pounds to go through the whole process for what was by now an aged 35-seat midibus, so it was stripped of anything useful and eventually went for scrap.

## Selkent Optare Delta DA1 (the first customer-order Delta to be delivered)

Optare's Delta was introduced in 1988, the first examples, as might be expected, being demonstrators — one in Optare livery and another wearing DAF corporate colours for the Hughes DAF dealership. The first Delta to be completed to the order of a customer was Selkent DA1 (F54 CWY).

I was asked to drive the bus to Blackpool for display at the 1989 National Coach Rally. It was to have been a one-way journey, as Selkent Managing Director Brian Constable would be attending and was due to take it to London with him at the day's end. With what was essentially a prototype with several London features, that plan was somewhat optimistic, as some changes were decided upon, and unexpectedly I had to do a return trip to Optare's factory at Cross Gates in Leeds. As I left Blackpool I thought I'd take the opportunity to pose my London steed with some of the locals, so I drove into Blackpool Transport's Rigby Road yard and took some photographs.

I found the bus very pleasing to drive, the automatic gearbox leaving the driver to concentrate on the road, and the excellent suspension gave a very comfortable ride. I wasn't so keen on the brakes, which needed a firm press and then seemed to work quite suddenly. This trait was, apparently, normal for a European bus, and one with which I was to become familiar in the ensuing years.

**A rare visit to Rigby Road by a new London bus saw the standard Blackpool Atlantean in danger of being outnumbered by Optares and not-so-new London buses.**

**The architecture of St George's Hall in Liverpool contrasts sharply with the Den Oudsten Alliance City B90.**

Much more worrying were the small catches holding the battery-access flap in place under the driver's window and which gave up the ghost on the M55. When cruising at the maximum governed speed of 50mph the flap slowly opened upwards, and as it did so, described an arc in the fresh air to my right. As I pulled onto the hard shoulder all I could think about was the possibility of a motorcyclist overtaking at just the wrong moment!

After a few minutes fiddling and tightening the offending catches I set off again. They must have worked loose because of vibration caused by a combination of speed and the concrete road surface. I had to stop twice or three times more on the motorways and reported the incidents upon my arrival at Optare. I've never heard of this problem affecting any other Delta, so the problem catches must have been sorted out.

## Den Oudsten Alliance City B90 in Liverpool (a 'one-off' in Britain)

Another Optare adventure, in 1992, was a little more public, in that I was asked to take a left-hand drive bus to Liverpool for a demonstration of low-floor buses. The vehicle was a Dutch Den Oudsten Alliance City, which had been loaned by Nord Zuid Hollandse, one of the railway-owned companies operating in the Amsterdam area. It had a DAF engine and ZF 4HP500 automatic transmission, similar to many new buses of the period. Noteworthy was the extensive use of polyester in the construction of the body, including front and rear bumpers, roof, front and rear assemblies and the side panels, which were bonded to the frame. On the journey to Liverpool I concluded that this 'plastic bus' was very similar to a Delta to drive. It was to be compared by Merseytravel against three other European low-floor buses — a Neoplan N4014 with an MAN engine, a Van Hool A300 with a side-mounted vertical DAF engine, and an MAN NL 202 with Berkhof 2000 bodywork.

I had been informed that early on the first day I would have a familiarisation run around the city-centre route, with only the salesmen from Optare for company. However, as soon as we got to our William Brown Street 'terminus' local people, including some on crutches and more than one in a wheelchair, thronged on board, and one of the salesmen signalled me to set off.

Driving a left-hand-drive bus around a city-centre circuit with a young council employee giving me directions was a truly frightening experience, aggravated by the mass of humanity seemingly squeezed into our bus. All this was on top of the fact that I was sitting 5ft or so to the right of my usual position with the (very low) platform way over to the left. Several lay-bys had been modified by the addition of temporary islands to the road side, so that test buses could drive in and pick up or set down, almost as if normal.

The Den Oudsten was about six months old and had

been in revenue-earning service, while the other three buses were all demonstrators. Each had a coloured board with a number so that the volunteer passengers could easily identify the buses when voting for them or merely passing comment. (I still have the Den Oudsten's red windscreen board in my collection.) Several months later an order was announced for Neoplans.

### Bova Futura FLC Express (the first Cummins-engined Futura in Britain)

In 1994 Optare Coach Sales imported the first Bova Futura in the country to be fitted with a Cummins 8.3-litre C300 engine instead of the usual DAF 11.63-litre unit, mated to a ZF automatic gearbox. It was intended for use as an express coach, economic operation being its main selling point. I was asked by Optare's Managing Director, Russell Richardson, to take the coach out for a test drive and report on my findings. The settings of the gearbox seemed to suit the Cummins engine very well, as it allowed brisk acceleration and provided smooth changes, both up and down. In all other respects the coach was a standard Bova Futura.

On another occasion I drove the Bova to another of my favourite photographic 'posing spots' for brochures, this being Temple Newsham House, a few miles to the east of Leeds. It was always fun taking a 12m coach down a narrow country lane and through the gate posts (less than 9ft apart) and see the faces of dog walkers trying to leave in their cars!

The Futura was already well known for being able to achieve an mpg figure in the low teens, owing to its slippery front end, so fitting an engine aimed primarily at economy should have provided a bonus in terms of fuel economy. In the event the Cummins-engined version seems to have faded away along with the Optare Coach Sales dealership, which had been set up when the company was in United Bus ownership. By contrast the DAF (now Paccar)-engined Futura, given occasional styling updates to keep it fresh, continues to sell well and, indeed, has recently celebrated its 25th anniversary.

### Scania L94/Carsa 10.75m (a 'one-off' in Britain, possibly the world)

During my 10 years providing print and promotional services to Scania Bus & Coach UK I often drove vehicles, many times to local scenic spots for photography.
On one occasion in 2004 I had to move 10 of Travel West Midlands' 11 articulated OmniCitys, on my own, to pose them for photography. Scania at that time offered a model for most sectors of the market, having recently introduced the N94/East Lancs OmniDekka, incorporating Scania's standard 'smiley' front panel, and the 12m single-deck L94, as well as a comprehensive range of coach chassis.

**The Bova Futura Express posed in the car park at Temple Newsham House.**

**The neat and stylish Carsa-bodied Scania N94, as yet unregistered, at Scania's Worksop premises.**

It was decided that the company was missing out on midibus sales, and as a result the 'Small Bus' was born. This employed the standard N94 modular underframe; the front and rear units were placed closer together, giving an overall length of 10.75m. A batch was built for Durham Travel Services' London Easylink operation, with East Lancs bodywork, followed by similar vehicles, now with the standard Scania front, for Nottingham. Unfortunately, after just four of the Easylink buses had been delivered, Durham Travel Services collapsed; however, all 14 eventually entered service in London, the remaining 10 doing so with East Thames Buses, which took over the DTS operation.

A dual-sourcing of bodybuilders had been planned for the midibus, and there duly appeared at Scania's Worksop premises an N94 bodied by Carsa, established as recently as 1998 and part of the Castrosua group, Spain's leading city-bus bodybuilder. I really liked the look of the bus, with its version of the Scania front, while inside it was very well finished, with close attention to detail, and could have been mistaken for a German product. I drove it several times around the premises, and there were none of the expected body rattles or squeaks.

The project seemed to end there, with no further sales of the OmniTown, as the 'Small Bus' had become, and the Carsa-bodied L94 remained the only one built. As far as I know it is unique, certainly in Britain and probably the world, there being few right-hand-drive markets. It found a buyer in The King's Ferry, at the time a keen Scania operator, for use on a regular transfer service. And it didn't even need a repaint!

# Seven decades of service

**Les Dickinson** lives and works in Cardigan, the home territory of the respected family firm of Richards Bros. Here he looks at the company's history.

*All photographs by Tony Moyes.*

When, in the early years of World War 2, haulier William Richards entered the passenger-carrying business, transporting workmen in small vans, he could scarcely have imagined how it would flourish, to the extent that seven decades later his descendants would be responsible for a fleet of no fewer than 70 vehicles operating throughout much of West Wales.

The first proper bus, bought in May 1943, was a Bedford OWB, built to wartime specification, while the operating base was a modest site in the village of Moylegrove, close to the town of Cardigan, in north Pembrokeshire. The original contract was for transporting workers to and from the Royal Naval Armaments Depot at Trecwn, and contracts for the military, notably the Royal Aircraft Establishment at Aberporth, continued to be important to the business throughout the 1950s and '60s. Over the years the company saw many operators come and go, most notably the mighty Western Welsh and also Crosville, which expanded into south Cardiganshire in the early 1970s but ultimately retreated from the area almost entirely. Richards has not only taken over several of the services once operated by these giants but has also bought out a number of smaller local operators, including Owen Williams of Cardigan in 1958 and Lewis Williams (Blue Glider) of St Dogmaels in 1972. In 1976 it took over Pioneer Motors of Newport, for which firm Reggie Richards, a son of the founder, had worked for many years. In August 1981 the Haverfordwest–St Davids service of Southampton-based Marchwood Motorways was acquired, while the most recent takeover, in 1998, involved the bus fleet and services of T. M. Daniels of Cardigan, though this firm retains its garage business.

Over the years Bedford remained the preferred marque, being purchased new and second-hand, with bodywork largely by Plaxton, Duple and Willowbrook. More than 100 have been operated by the Richards family, among them 12-seat Dormobiles and examples of the OWB, OB, SB, VAS,

**Over the years Richards has operated more than 100 Bedfords. They included this venerable OB, photographed in Fishguard in 1970, alongside a C5. Both were bodied by Duple, the OB having coach seats for 29 passengers, the C5 bus seats for 30.**

**This Weymann-bodied AEC Reliance had been new to Devon General in 1957 and was acquired by Richards in 1971. It is seen leaving Cardigan on the service to Tresaith.**

VAM, VAL and Y-series. The Y-series have been particularly numerous, numbering more than 60, and as recently as 2006 the fleet included a few stalwarts giving regular daily service. The last to be acquired by Richards — bought second-hand from another operator — had been new in 1988. Earlier second-hand purchases, during the 1950s and '60s included a Bristol LL, an Albion Nimbus and assorted Leylands, while an AEC Reliance arrived in 1971. There were also a few double-deckers, including a Bristol K6A, an AEC Regent V, some Leyland Titans and finally, in 1974, an AEC Bridgemaster. Following the demise of Bedford, purchases have mostly been of Volvo, DAF (favoured for a couple of dozen buses and coaches) or Dennis manufacture but have also included midibuses from Mercedes-Benz.

The fleet livery has seen many variations, although its evolution, one suspects, has been influenced by purchases from other operators. The company's traditional blue and maroon was eventually joined on the buses with some white relief, whilst the coaches generally wore rather more white. Precise application has generally been dictated by the particular body style, although for a time the livery made much use of stripes and lines. Eventually coaches became white with red, grey and black lettering, while buses adopted silver with a blue skirt and a red stripe — a scheme inspired by Optare's demonstration livery. In the 1990s, following a trend set in NBC days by National Welsh and South Wales, the company began applying the Welsh translation of its name – Brodyr Richards – to the offside of its vehicles. More recently continuing co-operation with local government has seen some new vehicles, for longer routes, branded 'TrawsCambria' and outshopped in a scheme which acknowledges the support of Ceredigion Council and the Welsh Office. A similar livery is worn by Arriva Cymru vehicles used on these routes, the operator of each individual vehicle being identifiable from the logo below one of the rearmost side windows.

As its name implies, Richards Bros remains a family-run business, although with its fleet of new and used vehicles it gives the impression of being a much bigger operator, and even the older vehicles are always turned out in immaculate condition, a credit to the company. It now has two major depots — one in Cardigan, which opened in 1984, the other at Newport (Pembrokeshire), opened in 1978 — each of which would dwarf the original premises in Moylegrove. Along with coach tours further afield, regular bus services are operated throughout West Wales, and although the original MoD work gradually faded away in the 1980s and '90s as the Government progressively wound down the various sites the company has built an equally important base of school contracts, transporting hundreds of schoolchildren each day. Indeed, it prides itself on its service to local communities, linking many otherwise isolated villages and on a number of its routes picking up and setting down on demand, in some cases even dropping passengers by their doorstep! Such is the bond between operator and community that many drivers and passengers are on first-name terms, and drivers are quick to notice if a regular passenger is not at his or her usual stop for the market-day bus.

In conclusion the author would like to acknowledge the assistance provided by Marteine Richards, one of the three brothers who now run the business, and with whom he had the good fortune to become acquainted when both were active members of the Cardigan Chamber of Trade. During three terms of office as Chairman the author could always rely on Marteine's help with Chamber activities. How many other bus-industry bosses get so actively involved with the communities that keep them in work?

*Left:* **Double-deckers have played but a small part in Richards' operations. The last was this former City of Oxford AEC Bridgemaster, pictured operating on a contract from RAE Aberporth in 1977.**

*Below:* **The Bedford Y-series was a popular choice in the Richards fleet of the 1970 and 1980s. This Willowbrook-bodied YRQ had been new to Yeoman of Canon Pyon in 1971. It is seen opposite Newport depot, where it has paused for a crew change while working the service between Cardigan and Haverfordwest in the summer of 1984.**

**_Above:_ An example of the bigger YRT — 11m long, compared with 10m for the YRQ — with 53-seat Duple Dominant bus bodywork passes through Newport in 1984. It had been new in 1976 to Maidstone Borough Council.**

**_Left:_ The rural nature of much of the company's operation is apparent from this view of a Willowbrook-bodied Bedford SB on a school run near Llanychaer in March 1993. The bus had been new 21 years earlier to the Oxfordshire Health Authority.**

**_Left:_ The first Optare Delta to be delivered to a Welsh operator entered service with Richards in September 1990. It is pictured in 1996 loading for Cardigan in the bus station at Haverfordwest.**

*Left:* **Five new Dennis Darts were purchased in the 1990s, among them this one with Plaxton Pointer bodywork, which entered service at the start of 1994. It is seen in Aberystwyth later that year.**

*Below:* **An ex-demonstration TransBus Enviro300 leaves Cardigan in the summer of 2004 on the hourly service to Haverfordwest. A 50-seater, it was the first Enviro300 to be completed.**

*Left:* **A number of new Optare products have been purchased by Richards in the 2000s, including Solos, Tempos and a Versa. This particular Solo had been an Optare demonstrator and is seen on the Cardigan–Llandysul service in 2005. It displays the company's clever website address — www.GoByBus.net — behind the rear wheel.**